D0547268

Inside China's Shadow Banking:
The Next Subprime Crisis?

Joe Zhang

Enrich Professional Publishing

Singapore • Hong Kong • Beijing • Honolulu

Published by

Enrich Professional Publishing, Inc.
Davies Pacific Center, 841 Bishop Street, Suite 208
Honolulu, HI, 96813
Website: www.enrichprofessional.com
A Member of Enrich Culture Group Limited

Hong Kong Office:
2/F, Rays Industrial Building, 71 Hung To Road, Kwun Tong, Kowloon, Hong Kong, China

China Office:
Rm 309, Building A, Central Valley, 16 Hai Dian Zhong Jie, Haidian District, Beijing, China

Singapore Office:
16L, Enterprise Road, Singapore 627660

English edition © 2014 by Enrich Professional Publishing, Inc.

Edited by Janet Cheng and Glenn Griffith

All rights reserved. This book, or parts thereof, may not be reproduced in any form or by any means, electronic or mechanical, including photocopying, recording or any information storage and retrieval system now known or to be invented, without prior written permission from the Publisher.

ISBN (Hardback)   978-1-62320-016-9
ISBN (Paperback)   978-1-62320-017-6

Enrich Professional Publishing is an independent globally-minded publisher focusing on the economic and financial developments that have revolutionized New China. We aim to serve the needs of advanced degree students, researchers, and business professionals who are looking for authoritative, accurate, and engaging information on China.

This publication is designed to provide accurate and authoritative information in regard to the subject matter covered. It is sold with the understanding that the publisher is not engaged in rendering legal, accounting, or other professional services. If legal advice or other expert assistance is required, the services of a competent professional person should be sought.

This book is based on facts and the author's understanding of the facts. It has been written in good faith. In several cases, names have been hidden or masked in order to avoid embarrassment for the persons involved.

Investment is a risky game, and neither the author nor the publisher will accept any responsibility for losses as a result of reading this book or acting on its views.

Printed in Hong Kong.

Dedicated to my 55 colleagues at

Wansui Micro Credit Company in Guangzhou.

You are wonderful.

Contents

Foreword

Shadow Banking: China's New Frontier

What is shadow banking? Different people have different definitions. But one thing we all agree on is this: shadow banking represents the wide-ranging and sometimes complex financial activities outside the traditional banking activities of deposit-taking and lending.

From 2008 to 2009, the global financial crisis pushed shadow banking to the center of the storm. Some people even maintained that shadow banking was the very culprit of the crisis! Whatever the truth, there is no doubt that shadow banking has become a very crucial part of our daily lives. According to The Financial Stability Board, the total value of shadow banking had exceeded USD67 trillion in the 26 major countries it surveyed as of the end of 2011.This was roughly 25% of these countries' total financial assets, or 200% of their GDP.

In China, shadow banking started with a low base but it has grown at exponential rates. Between 2008 and 2012, its size tripled to RMB20 trillion, equivalent to 20% of the country's GDP. The trend now seems unstoppable.

Broadly speaking, there are three groups of participants in China's shadow banking. First, there are the banks which offer various wealth management products both on and off their balance sheets. Second, there are the non-bank financial institutions, which include microcredit firms, guarantee companies, trust companies, finance companies, and leasing companies. And third, there are the curb-market financiers which mainly act as financial intermediaries for small businesses and underprivileged consumers.

The rapid growth of shadow banking in recent years owes much to the credit tightening by the central People's Bank of China. But there is a more fundamental reason. Small and medium-sized businesses cannot really count on regular banks to meet their ever-growing and complex financial needs. Many of them find regular banking services inflexible as well as insufficient. Shadow banking has risen to the challenge to fill the gap. On the other hand, the growth of shadow banking has posed competition for the banks. The banks must shape up in order to maintain their market share.

That said, shadow banking is more opaque than regular banking, and for good reason. It is subject to different sets of regulations, and enforcement of those regulations can be patchy. It lacks standardization and its products come in different forms and shapes. After all, shadow banking entails innovation and creativity, a hallmark it acquired from its origin.

In a way, investment banks sit comfortably between regular banking and shadow banking. A better description may be that the three blocks overlap each other. As a Hong Kong subsidiary of a major Chinese investment bank, Haitong International Securities Group sits at the forefront of shadow banking.

After working 17 years at foreign investment banks in Hong Kong, 11 of which were at UBS, Joe Zhang took the plunge into the Chinese microcredit industry two years ago. His personal experiences are interesting as well as educational.

We are pleased to present his book to the investors and clients of Haitong International, although we may not agree with all of his views.

Lin Yong
Chief Executive Officer
Haitong International Securities Group Limited

Introduction

My Personal Journey in China's Shadow Banking Industry

After working for foreign banks in Hong Kong for 17 years, I resigned as Deputy Head of China Investment Banking at UBS in June 2011. I did not go to greener pastures. Instead, I became Chairman of Wansui Micro Credit in Guangzhou, a small "shadow bank."

In January 2012, the Microcredit Association of China named me a "Microcredit Person of the Year."

I fell in love with microcredit three years ago. Since then, I have made friends and enemies in the industry through my aggressive campaigns to right the wrongs of the industry's regulations, change the public's attitude towards the industry, and grow the firms I invested in.

Shadow banking in China takes many forms and shapes. While its rapid growth is a result of financial repression, it meets genuine and legitimate needs and wants. The discrimination imposed on the sector by the government and the public is hurting the struggling small businesses and underprivileged consumers.

However, I grew tired, and disenchanted. Moreover, I started to see the bigger picture. It is China's negative real interest rates that caused the rapid growth of shadow banking such as the 6,000-plus microcredit firms, the thousands and thousands of curb-market operators, and the countless wealth management products at banks and trust companies.

In the past two decades, negative real interest rates and

runaway credit growth have reinforced each other, creating the biggest credit bubble on the planet.

This bubble is likely to become the origin of the next global crisis, if it is not carefully deflated.

In the past three years, I have invested a lot of time and money in China's microcredit sector. But I still have not figured out how to operate such a business in a scalable way. Maybe I will never succeed, but I want to make sure that I have learned something along the way.

Joe Zhang
Hong Kong, May 2013

email: joe@chinamezz.com
blog: www.blog.sina.com.cn/joezhang33

1
Chapter

Plunging into Shadow Banking

On June 20, 2011, as I walked out of the offices of UBS Investment Bank, located in the grand IFC Mall in Hong Kong, I was feeling a sense of pride and excitement.

I had done it again!

This was the second time that I had walked away from a sought-after job from the same bank. Just over five years earlier, in March 2006, I had resigned from my position as Head of China Research at the same bank to run a sprawling government-controlled conglomerate company with more than 1,000 employees in several cities. That company, Shenzhen Investment Limited (0604 HK), has had its stock listed on the stock exchange of Hong Kong since 1997.

As its Chief Operating Officer and a board director, I probably made a difference to the sleepy company in the more than two years that I was there. The Chairman and CEO of Shenzhen Investment Limited had given me considerable managerial autonomy. Thanks to a bullish stock market and aggressive restructuring, the company's stock price had seen a six-fold increase between 2006 and 2008. The company sold several non-core businesses, including cable TV operations, power plants, toll roads, and manufacturing plants, to focus only on real estate development. Taking advantage of the surging stock price, it had raised US$350 million in fresh equity and several billion dollars of cheap long-term loans.

Bloomberg and many media outlets had written feature stories about the company's transformation and my contributions. *Institutional Investor* magazine even carried a cover story about me and my work. However, government-controlled businesses are always subject to political and social constraints. For example, these companies find it unacceptable to fire employees even when their workforce is clearly bloated. Employees' performance assessments are generally just formalities. Moreover, these companies are slow to make business decisions. Soon, I found out that I was unable to do what was needed to really transform the business, and that sticking around would be just a waste of time. After all, the management team had probably picked low-hanging fruit in the company's restructuring.

In late September 2008, as Lehman Brothers was collapsing, I was hired back by UBS as deputy head of its top-ranked China investment banking unit, to help corporate clients raise money through initial public offerings (IPOs) and bond sales. UBS and Goldman Sachs were the only two foreign banks who were licensed to operate in China's domestic capital markets. The so-called A-share market had seemed an oasis in light of the chaos in the global capital markets outside China. I was to work in both the A-share market and the international capital markets. I also co-headed the real estate banking team in Asia. That seemed more interesting to me.

Chasing Deals as a Banker

However, struggling to dig themselves out of the subprime crisis, global investment banks faced a very difficult operating environment as their regulators and shareholders had become ever more assertive and critical. In hindsight, the three years between 2009 and 2011 were something of a renaissance, or maybe just a false dawn, for the investment banking industry, at least in Asia, since deal flows rebounded nicely from the trough in late 2008 and early 2009.

But the job of an investment banker is very different from that of a research analyst. I must say that I did not enjoy chasing deals, particularly with the people I did not like much. Knowing that I probably had built a reasonable retirement nest egg and that I had a simple lifestyle, I gradually itched to take some risks again.

Since mid-2010, I've kept my eye on China's fast-growing microcredit industry and visited quite a few players. I quickly fell in love with them. I even had UBS sponsor a pawnshop to go public on the stock exchange of Hong Kong. Pawnshops are similar to microcredit companies though they are regulated by the Ministry of Public Security and the Ministry of Commerce, while microcredit companies are licensed and supervised by the Finance Offices of local governments.

Now, I was walking out of UBS again, not for greener pastures, but to become Chairman of Wansui Microcredit Company in Guangzhou, the capital city of Guangdong Province.

Wansui Microcredit Company was a small business with 50-some employees handing out small loans to mom-and-pop stores and cash-starved consumers who had long been neglected by banks. In recent years, the field of microcredit had become fashionable, not only because of the public's disappointment with bureaucratic banks, but also because of the sensation created by Muhammad Yunus, a Bangladeshi banker, who had won the Nobel Peace Prize in 2006 for his work in this field.

After all, running your own show is always a cool fantasy, particularly for investment bankers who endure the daily grind, and receive public criticism as the culprits for the global subprime crisis.

The irony was that, at that time, no one, least of all me, had thought that I was indeed taking the plunge into the subprime credit sector, albeit not the U.S. one.

A Successful Detective

As I got on a through-train in Kowloon to head for Guangzhou around lunchtime, I received a text message from a friend telling me that my move into microcredit was hitting the Chinese internet, and that dozens of websites had carried my story. Even Reuters and Bloomberg had reported it. I started to receive telephone calls from people I knew as well as from journalists. *Economic Observer*, a leading Chinese-language business newspaper in Beijing, splashed a full-page story on its front page the next day called "Joe Zhang's Microcredit Dream."

Almost all the newspapers in Hong Kong printed stories the next day about my becoming a loan shark. I guess another investment banker's move would not have attracted this much interest in the media, but I had gained some notoriety in my 18 years in Hong Kong, due partly to my making waves at Shenzhen Investment Limited, and partly to my being a whistleblower on three cases of corporate fraud in 2001 and 2002 while I was a research analyst. One of the listed companies that I wrote negative reports about, Greencool Technology (8056 HK), sued me and UBS for defamation in the Hong Kong High Court. About six months later, we settled out of court. I became the only research analyst in the history of Hong Kong to have had that experience. Less than two years after we settled the suit, Greencool went belly up, and its chairman, Gu Chujun, was sentenced to 18 years in prison for tax evasion and several other crimes.

Another company also listed in Hong Kong, Euro-Asia Agricultural (Holdings) Company Limited (0932 HK), threatened to sue me and UBS for libel after I told a large number of fund managers that the company's accounts were significantly inflated which sent its stock down 18 percent in one day in 2001. Coincidentally, the chairman of Euro-Asia, Yang Bin, who in 2002 was made the first Chief Executive of North Korea's special economic zone, *Sinuiju*, was also sentenced by China to an 18-year jail term, and his company went bust in 2002. Sadly, this all happened not before Yang and his cronies had made public threats to my life.

These two episodes had taught me a lesson, and I learned how to protect myself from corporate fraudsters. In 2004, I spotted strange irregularities at a food processing company. Though I took many fund managers to visit the company's operations afterwards and told them about my doubts and concerns, I did not write research reports about the company. Several years later, the food company went bankrupt, and I was not surprised.

In December 1998, I was abruptly fired by HSBC Securities as Head of China Research, after *South China Morning Post* reported my comment that a Yankee Bond to be issued by the Chinese Ministry of Finance in early 1999 was a "lose-lose proposition." HSBC and Goldman Sachs were the sponsors of the bond deal.

In my view, the massive media coverage of my change of career to microcredit told me two things.

First, the media (and the public) regarded microcredit as something of an underdog, only slightly more respectable than perhaps massage parlors or nightclubs.

Second, they thought investment bankers, particularly senior ones, were fat cats while microfinanciers were the poor cousins.

Interestingly, I was about to find out that the public was probably right. Maybe it was another case of the wisdom of the crowd?

After the Communist Party took office in China in 1949, the party quickly nationalized all sorts of businesses, not to mention the financial sector. While starvation in the late 1970s had forced the government to relax regulations on the less strategic sectors such as manufacturing, retail businesses, and textiles since the early 1980s, the government had maintained tight controls over the financial sector.

Ideologically, the government and the public regarded microcredit and the high interest rates associated with the sector as immoral and dangerous...and disruptive to the mainstream banking industry.

Only in 2008, after years of debate and small-scale experimentation did the People's Bank of China and the China Banking Regulatory Commission (CBRC) jointly issue a decree to formally recognize, and to legalize, the microcredit sector.

The decree had opened the floodgates. Since 2008, over 5,000 microcredit companies have been set up with the approval of local governments. Wansui, being one of the first to obtain a license in Guangzhou, was seen as better managed and more reputable.

> **// Since 2008, over 5,000 microcredit companies have been set up with the approval of local governments. //**

First Day at Work

Two hours after leaving Kowloon and UBS in Central, Hong Kong, I arrived at the Guangzhou East Rail Station. A young driver, Wenchuan Li, from Wansui picked me up. After driving for another hour, we entered Huadu District of Guangzhou Province, the home of Wansui.

While Wansui's offices are bright, clean, and tidy, they are unbelievably simple, only equipped with cheap desks and PCs. I even suspected that those PCs had been bought from secondhand markets as their makes and sizes were all different. Though I had visited these offices on my previous visits, I still could not help but notice that Wansui, in a bid to cut costs, did not even install an air conditioner in the meeting room. In summer, Guangzhou can be brutally hot, as was the case on my first day at work.

I liked the people at Wansui. They all seemed very upbeat and happy. Chairman Xiaoqin Jiang, an elegant lady, who looked much younger than her age of 50, had founded the company in early 2009, after quitting her job at the Bank of Communications in 2008. Jiang had worked for China Construction Bank in Jiangsu and then Guangdong for over two decades, and she eventually became Head of the Bank of Communications in neighboring Foshan City. I had met her on my two visits to Wansui in 2010.

In the middle of the night one early June day in 2011, Jiang and Wansui's general manager Yu Wen woke me up by calling to say that Jiang had become unwell and was in need of an extended period of rest. They had invited me to replace her as chairman and legal representative. They strongly urged me to travel to Guangzhou to discuss the transition with them. After thinking about it for just a day, I accepted the job.

As I learned a year later, there was a much more complex and syndical reason for her relinquishing her job.

Still, I never anticipated the eventual bitter power struggle with her that happened a year later. This struggle ended with my firing her in a heavy-handed manner which was not my usual style.

2

Chapter

Great Expectations

Unlike Mohammad Yunus, the Bangladeshi banker, I was just a selfish, or self-interested, banker. While I am sometimes idealistic about social issues, my primary motivation for leaving my senior banking job at UBS for Wansui Microcredit was to build on past successes.

But I also wanted to hopefully make a lot of money for myself, although I knew that I was taking on a lot of risks.

I thought I had analyzed the industry carefully. I thought I was better equipped than most startup entrepreneurs.

I do not have to worry about finances for my family, as I have saved enough money for my retirement and children's education. And Wansui did not appear a risky bet, having been in operation successfully for more than two consecutive years.

In the 1980s, I worked a few years at the central People's Bank of China in Beijing, and had maintained some good connections there. Equally important, many of my friends and former schoolmates now worked in the government and the financial industry. That was particularly relevant for the microcredit sector.

Until about 10 years ago, Huadu District was a rural county. After the new Guangzhou Baiyun airport moved to Huandu, and several automobile companies (including Dongfeng Auto and Nissan) built plants there, it became more prosperous. Today, Huadu has a population of one million and an area of 961 square kilometers.

Though Wansui was the only licensed microfinance firm in Huadu, we had to compete with over 30 banks that, apart from taking deposits and making corporate lending, had started to dip their toes into SME lending (small and medium-sized enterprises) and even consumer finance. Indeed, every major bank has operations in Huadu.

Ping An Insurance Group sells microcredit throughout the nation, including in Huadu. Essentially, Ping An sells a credit default swap to its partner banks.

That kind of swap works like this: Ping An identifies qualified customers, and provides its partner bank (e.g. ICBC Bank) with a money-back guarantee. ICBC charges customers an interest rate of 30% per annum, and pays 23% to Ping An for a money-back guarantee. Thus ICBC pockets the 7% difference as a "risk-free" loan. Nationwide, Ping An is said to have a principal loan book of RMB20 billion via credit default swaps. Guangzhou Rural Business Bank and Minsheng Bank were also our competitors.

Of foreign banks, Standard Chartered Bank has a branch office in the same building as Wansui, making nothing but loans to small businesses. Their interest rates are lower than those charged by Wansui, but they are more demanding regarding the quality of customers.

When I became chairman of Wansui, regulations did not allow us to branch into other geographical areas outside Huadu. But we did not complain about that particular rule, as Huadu was a big enough place, and it seemed as if our capability to find enough good customers and fully utilize our loanable funds was still limited.

We had three outlets in the three biggest towns of Huadu handling customer services. We employed 50 people (compared to the industry average of 8 employees per institution). Our paid-in capital was RMB150 million (compared to the industry average of RMB100 million) and China Development Bank had lent us RMB75 million on a two-year basis. In comparison, about half of microcredit companies did not get any bank financing at all.

Skeletons in the Closet

When I joined Wansui, we had lent to 1,700 customers. Our average loan size was RMB130,000. Most of our loans went to small businesses as we had de-emphasized consumer lending. That average figure masks two large loans lent out when Wansui got started in April 2009: one was RMB20 million which was loaned to a fish farm (Luye Fishing), and the other was a RMB5 million loan to a furniture retailer (Hong Da). Ironically, both borrowers defaulted a year after I joined Wansui. While both loans were collateralized, foreclosure had become very difficult in the case of the fish farm, as multiple lenders had to fight for the dwindling value of a factory built on rural land in Huadu, and its land use rights stated that that site could only be used for industrial purposes. Shoddy due diligence work and wishful thinking on the part of Wansui management were to blame.

In the case of the second delinquent loan, we had repossessed its rental property in a Huadu village and were using it as our extended offices.

These two painful losses forced Wansui to focus on loans of smaller sizes. But habits die hard.

Just after I joined Wansui, Jiang and the team had lent RMB20 million to Hudete Air-Con, a small air conditioner manufacturer that trumpeted its environmentally friendly air conditioners and boasted that it was in the queue for an IPO in the domestic A-share market.

Jiang and another manager of Wansui decided to lend RMB20 million to the company at a preferential rate for an unusually long maturity (two years). It was clearly a sweetheart deal for Hudete, but a high cost and high risk deal for Wansui.

I did not know of this deal until after I joined. What shocked me most was that two senior managers at Wansui had accepted stock options personally from Hudete. The prospect of Hudete's IPO and a tidy profit for the two senior managers personally if the IPO were to materialize had clearly influenced their lending decisions.

I was furious. I gave both the two senior managers a warning, and taught them the concepts of impropriety and conflict of interest, demanding that they recall the loan. Fortunately for Wansui, Hudete repaid the loan on schedule, after a bank extended a bigger loan to them. After Wansui recalled the loans in stages in mid-2012, Huadete's prospects seemed to darken, and it shelved its plan to apply for an IPO.

In post-mortem, we discovered that everything that could have gone wrong had gone wrong with respect to Huadete Air-Con's loan. To start with, Wansui's management had a conflict of interest at a personal level. The two-year loan was mispriced at only 6% per annum, compared to Wansui's average lending rate of 20% to 24%. The maturity was also unusually long: two years, compared to Wansui's average loan maturity of 6 to 9 months.

Secondly, our credit officers took the company's plan to go public too seriously. Two decades of IPO euphoria in China had made everyone believe that going public was the surefire path to riches. Of course, many IPO aspirants never make it to the finish-line of the stock exchange. Such companies bleed to death on the way to the finish-line.

Finally, the business model of such a simple manufacturer in a sector with massive overcapacity is often flawed. This is because they always have to invest more money to make more money. They cannot afford to stop the R&D process, and have to deal with ever-growing marketing expenses, as they have become too dependent on these things to stay afloat. In other words, their cash flows are often problematic, and their free cash flows are even more problematic.

Huadete was already geared at 80% at the time Wansui made the loan in June 2010. The gearing ratio had grown since then. Wansui's lending officers took Huadete management's enthusiasm, diligence, and commitment as evidence of the company's great future, while de-emphasizing the weak economics in the business model itself. In Warren Buffett's words, "When the reputation of a terrible business meets the reputation of a good business manager, it is the former that will stand."

A few months prior to that shocking discovery of the dubious loan to Hudete Air-Con, Jiang had wanted to come back to work at Wansui as she stated that she had fully recovered from her illness. Given her founder status and her experience, I agreed. She wanted to act as the checks-and-balances on Wansui's general manager, Yu Wen, a man she had recruited for Wansui on day one. I thought it was a sensible idea, so I created a position for her (Chief Operating Officer). Both she and Yu would have the signing authority.

A Nice Little Business

Microcredit companies are permitted to charge customers as much as 4 times the bank's prime lending rate, meaning 24% per annum (as prime is around 6%). Some firms charge extra fees to bypass regulation, but not Wansui. We feel that 24% is already very high, and charging higher rates would only increase risks. Indeed, we consciously lowered our lending rates when demand was slack in the first half of 2012.

You could not fault Jiang and the team for having no ambitions. While some of the things were done far short of best practices, they did make efforts. From day one (March 2009), Wansui's accounts have been audited by Grant Thornton whose audit fees are higher than those charged by local shops. In 2009,

Wansui made a profit of about RMB5 million, and in 2010, the profit reached RMB19 million, and in 2011, RMB25 million. However, all this was due to the lack of an adequate provision for bad debts. In 2012, the company took a specific charge of RMB8 million for several dead loans, in addition to RMB2.5 million for the general provision for bad debts. If the tax office were to permit it, Wansui's net profits would have been all but wiped out by bad loan write-offs.

Our financial data for 2012 looked like this:

1. Average loan balance: RMB231 million
2. Sales: RMB69 million
3. 5.56% business tax and surcharges (RMB3.8 million)
4. Labor costs for 55 employees (RMB12 million)
5. 2% general provisions for bad debts
6. Expenses such as rents, utilities, etc. (RMB5 million)
7. 25% enterprise income tax (RMB8.6 million)
8. Net profits: RMB26 million
9. Return on shareholders' funds: about 17%

In most provinces, regulators have a strange rule that does not allow microcredit firms to retain earnings. So, they have to distribute all their earnings to shareholders. Not that I mind it. But these firms will forever be small shops, unless they go through a tedious and time-consuming set of procedures to recapitalize.

Like in other industries, to get anything done, whether you want to recapitalize your microcredit company, or open a branch office, or change a shareholder structure, or get a tax concession, there is inevitably a certain amount of pleading, begging, wining-and-dining, golfing, and other backscratching to be done with regulatory officials. On several occasions, I lost my cool with these officials when arguing about the stupidity of the regulations and the officials' reluctance to do anything for us little guys. Some officials envy business people and deliberately make their lives difficult, and some go out of their way to extract personal benefits.

Within the local government, the Finance Office (*jinrong bangongshi* 金融辦公室) or Finance Department (*jinrongju* 金融局) is not to be confused with the powerful Treasury Department (*caizhengju* 財政局) which is responsible for the government's budget. It used to be an ad hoc and obscure office which produced speeches for local politicians and coordinated inconsequential matters between banks, insurance companies, fund houses, and securities companies, as the regulation of these institutions rested with the respective departments in the central government. But in 2008, luck smiled on the local governments' Finance Offices. They were given the responsibility to license and supervise the microcredit industry. This newly-acquired power did not go unnoticed. As a frustrated manager of a microcredit company only half-jokingly put it, "In 2008, these officials suddenly moved their offices to golf courses."

Maybe I am not chairman material as I never play golf and never take anyone to a karaoke bar. The most that I will do for officials is to take them to an ordinary lunch or dinner. This is a habit I acquired from my two decades of work at foreign banks. I told employees at Wansui on numerous occasions, "If what you want to do appears in the newspapers tomorrow, and you will not feel embarrassed, then go ahead and do it. Otherwise, think twice."

In a heavily polluted business environment, I do not know how much of that preaching has stuck with my colleagues.

Apathetic Regulators

Wansui was capitalized at RMB150 million, and regulation allowed us to borrow only 50% of our paid-in capital. We are not allowed to take deposits or borrow from the interbank market or other sources. That is very restrictive and unfair to us, in light of banks' leverage ratios and the longer leash afforded to leasing companies (10 times) and guarantee companies (also 10 times). Even local credit unions are subjected to a generous cap on their gearing. The restrictions placed upon us are largely due to our humble status. Remember we were only legalized in 2008.

I did not want to give up without a good fight. Leveraging off my media influence and my contacts in the banking industry and the government, I lobbied the government to relax this restriction for the sake of the economy and our underprivileged customers.

You cannot believe how inefficient some of China's regulations of the microcredit industry and, indeed, of many other sectors, are. For example, as a small firm, we have three layers of regulators: the Huadu District Department of Development and Reforms, the Huangzhou City Finance Department, and the Guangdong Provincial Government Finance Department. They often disagree on things big or small. We are often stuck in the middle. When we want to get anything done (even open a small branch or change a minority shareholder), we have to apply to the district government, and then the city government and finally the provincial government. You can lose patience quickly if you do not practice *Tai Chi* and take deep breaths.

One of the reasons why I plunged into this sector was because I already knew the harsh restrictions. How much worse could they get? What was my downside? I thought that these tough restrictions were impossible to sustain, and once a relaxation took place, we could embrace a huge business opportunity. However, I underestimated the intransigence of the regulators and their apathy. Why should anyone care?

One day, I went to see a senior regulator in Guangzhou, trying to convince him to increase our leverage cap from 0.5 times paid-in capital to 1 times. After lengthy discussions about the norm in other countries and experimental relaxation in Chongqing, and the limited risks of deregulation, he said, "You just want to make more money. Microcredit firms are already making a lot of money. How much more money do you want to make?"

Stunned, I responded, "What is wrong with making more money? I am a businessman. Only when we make a lot of money can we finance more customers, and create more jobs!"

He shot back. "That is none of my business! I have my superiors. I cannot make that decision."

I have engaged in this type of discussion and confrontation elsewhere.

As a panel speaker at the annual conference of The China Microcredit Association held in Beijing on January 8, 2012, I even made the mistake of offending the audience by saying that China was poor because we Chinese were stupid. "We always shoot ourselves in the foot." Those remarks really upset several officials who had just presented me with a prestigious award of "Microcredit Person of the Year."

At the tea break, a wise friend told me to put things in perspective. China is a country with a 5,000-year history, she continued, "It is naïve of you to think you can change something in a matter of months or even years." I sighed, and reflected on my other frustrations.

That afternoon, I was scheduled to speak to a large group of students at the Graduate School of the People's Bank of China on the very topic of the microcredit industry. From 1983 to 1986, I studied at the Graduate School before I got a job at the central bank as a regulatory official in 1986. It was always a warm feeling when I went back to visit that small campus. But I felt tense that day, and told my audience that China was hopeless. I continued, "In 1986 when I graduated from this place, my degree thesis was *The Path to Interest Rate Liberalization*. Twenty-six years later, you are still writing degree theses about the same topic. In the 1980s, the government made us believe that liberalization of interest rates and, indeed, the Renminbi was only 5 years away. Those five years have never ended. The five-year targets have become constant rolling targets."

Lending Like a Private Equity Investor

At Wansui, we apply private equity methods to lending. As we focus on business loans rather than consumer loans, we analyze and predict cash flows carefully. If you walk in our office and ask for a loan to finance, say, your holiday in South Africa, we would politely ask you to go to another institution, even though you have a big house as collateral. Our approach to business is quite different from most other firms. We do not just sit in the office, waiting for customers to call. We assign three or five streets or villages to each credit officer. They proactively go out and visit prospective customers. Before customers ask for a loan, our credit officer should have done a reasonable amount of due diligence.

We emphasize consumer experience. Repeat customers are a very important phenomenon, so are customer referrals. As we serve repeat customers, our cost of loan appraisals declines sharply. As our employees have learned, walk-in customers are, on average, of lower quality credit.

For loans above RMB300,000, we demand collateral (usually real estate or the ownership of a factory or a business), and for loans below that threshold, we want a guarantee from a qualified person (who may own real estate or have a high income job). We emphasize cash flows and de-emphasize collateral and guarantees. If a loan has to be repaid by selling collateral or calling the guarantor, it means that our credit officers have done a bad job at credit evaluation.

Three Goals

Apart from lobbying for the regulator to lift the cap on our gearing, three other tasks are high on my agenda.

(1) Becoming a loan arranger for banks
I knew that several Chinese banks had set up such a program with microfinanciers in Shenzhen, Shanghai, and a few other cities. At Wansui, we want to replicate their model. Becoming a Lending Assistant is crucial in significantly boosting our capability, and improving our profitability.

(2) Loan securitization
Once your loan portfolio reaches a certain size, and you have largely run out of loanable funds, you can package your loans in parcels, and sell them to banks. This can boost your profitability as essentially you will be selling your services of originating new loans. Several banks have conducted loans securitization with microfinance firms. Wansui wants to imitate their success.

(3) Contract management
We believe that exporting our management expertise will be a triumph of dedication over fast bucks. In our industry, many firms find it much easier to make a small number of big loans than make a large number of small loans. At Wansui, we have learned this the hard way. Smaller loans are not only safer for our portfolio, but also more profitable, and more meaningful to the economy. Even before I joined Wansui, several microfinance operators had asked Wansui to manage their microcredit businesses. In late 2011, Wansui sent senior manager Wei He plus two experienced credit officers to Chengde City, Hunan Province, to manage Shuangxing, a government-controlled microcredit firm capitalized at RMB200 million.

For several years, we wanted to turn Wansui into a village

bank so that we would be able to take deposits. However, frustrations with regulators had convinced us that we would be far better off without the overbearing supervision of the China Banking Regulatory Commission.

Banks Pay Lip Service

Chinese banks understand the critical importance of agriculture and SMEs, but have done little thus far to help them. The fact that free market interest rates are 5 to 7 times higher than prime lending rates speaks volumes about the banks' inactivity and ineffectiveness. Why do banks not lend to SMEs and agriculture? I believe this stems from their ownership, governance, and cost structure. Farmers and SMEs complain that banks are inflexible (their loans assessment time-consuming), and too demanding (when it comes to collateral, loan size, and documentation) and that they have a culture of avoiding trouble (No one gets the blame for losing money on China Railways). Whenever credit tightening starts, the agricultural sector and SMEs suffer the most.

Interest Rates Are Not the Issue

How can a normal business survive on a high interest rate of around 26% a year? Think about this: private equity funds, hedge funds, and investment banks routinely demand an internal rate of return above 25%, and they have little trouble finding target projects. Indeed, they are often spoiled for choice. If these investors cut the average size of their investment tickets

> **//** Smaller loans are not only safer, but also more profitable, particularly when you are dealing with repeat customers. **//**

to our average loan size of RMB130,000 from, say, USD10 million, I am sure they will be swamped. Smaller loans are not only safer, but also more profitable, particularly when you are dealing with repeat customers as we are.

Think also about this: the usual interest rate banks globally charge credit card balances is around 30% to 40%, irrespective of economic cycles. They never have a shortage of willing takers for their money.

At Wansui, our usual microfinance customers are small businesses which have been neglected by banks. We are often their only place to go. Interest rates are not the key issue, but the availability of money is. If we charge customers 25% per annum for our money, and they recycle the money three or four times a year, they find the interest rate affordable, particularly considering the tedious procedures, the long waiting period, uncertainties, and even extra expenses associated with bank borrowing (kickbacks).

3
Chapter

Friends in High Places

In the first few weeks of my work at Wansui, I was busy getting to know the company's operations and our staff. I also lived a life like a hero or celebrity. Some employees had previously read my Chinese language book, *The Confessions of a Stock Analyst*. Many colleagues were excited by the extraordinary media coverage of their new chairman.

A Celebrity at Work

In those first few weeks, I was also swamped with requests for interviews from the media, as well as visits by curious bankers, private equity investors, academics, officials, and rivals.

Two groups of visitors are worth mentioning here: government officials and microfinanciers from other cities. Some government officials wanted to know my views on how to boost and better regulate the sector. Some had also invited me to invest in (or set up) microcredit institutions in their cities. The other types of visitors were microcredit companies' managers or prospective investors. They were curious, as well as pleased, that a senior investment banker would join their ranks. They liked the media attention for their industry.

I was proud to show visitors around our simple branch offices (which I thought were cool) and prouder to treat them to lunch in our conference room. The room was not equipped with an air conditioner and it was very hot in the summer. In several cases, I deliberately took some visiting bankers and "white shoe" private equity people to my simple and austere hotel (New Donghao) for meals. I must say I was pumped up, and very excited. I told some visitors that it was the first time in the past two decades that I had stayed in such a budget hotel. I felt good.

Like a celebrity person, I was invited to speak about microcredit at many conferences or internal meetings around the country. One of my carefully prepared and passionate speeches attracted millions of readers, and was reprinted by numerous newspapers and websites. It was entitled "Give High Cost Finance Full Respect" and in it, I talked about the financial inequality in China, and the critical importance of giving underprivileged people equal access to finance. In the speech, I had blasted the prejudices many in the government and the public held against microcredit. Instantly, I had become the undisputed spokesman for the 5,000 licensed microcredit companies around the country, and many others who were aspiring to set up such shops.

More importantly, many unlicensed private financers felt delighted that someone influential was on their side.

Champion of the Underdogs

In recent years, the government had allowed unlicensed citizens to lend to each other as long as they do not take deposits, or do not raise funds from more than 50 parties. However, unlicensed entities and individuals still face huge regulatory risks when and if fundraising is involved. A few years earlier, a Zhejiang-based company controlled by a young lady, Wu Ying, was involved in fundraising from more than 50 parties and unfortunately some of these investments and loans had gone sour. Under pressure from creditors (many of whom were individuals), Wu was given a death sentence by the court and she appealed the ruling. The high court subsequently gave her a suspended death sentence in May 2012, after her appeals. The protracted court case divided China as many had blamed the government for unfair, unjust, and arbitrary regulation of the sector.

Partly because of my many speeches and blog articles, I was invited to give a special lecture at Beijing University on the topic of microcredit in April 2012, and to sit on the Expert Panel for

SME Finance under the auspices of the All-China Confederation of Industry and Commerce since September 2012.

After a few weeks of my honeymoon with the media and visitors, I had to get down to real business. I identified two immediate priorities.

My first goal was to convince at least one bank to accept Wansui as a microcredit origination agent.

And my second goal was to find ways to securitize our loan portfolio since we could not count on regulators to lift the cap on our gearing ratios any time soon.

I quickly started my marketing campaign. First, I identified the heads of major commercial banks to visit. In July 2011, I visited Lu Xin, a deputy CEO of a top bank in its Beijing head office. Lu and I both studied at the Graduate School of the People's Bank, and while at the cozy Graduate School we played basketball together a few times. He had read my story on the internet, and was curious about my grand plan. However, he said he was not directly responsible for SME lending and suggested that I approach the local branches of his bank in Guangzhou. After all, he said that microcredit was too negligible due to his bank's size. Though we had a good chat about the strange world in which we lived and some common friends, I sensed that microcredit was not high on his agenda. A few weeks later, in an alumni dinner in Hong Kong which both Lu and I attended, I raised the issue again, but it was quickly sidelined by other dinner conversations.

My next stop was to visit Ma Weihua, CEO of China Merchants Bank Group. Ma, 62, is a charismatic statesman in the industry. We both worked at the People's Bank of China head office in the 1980s. He was an assistant to Governor Chen Muhua and I was a junior manager at the bank. On several occasions, he had asked me to have a first crack at drafting speeches for Chen. And I respected and liked him a lot. Ma was delighted to see me after so many years. During my 11 years at UBS in the past, I was a research analyst and then a banker but I did not cover the financial institutions sector which meant that I never saw him beyond cocktail parties or the office lobby.

Ma was very generous to me with his time. I took Wansui's Yu Wen to the meeting. On Ma's side at the meeting were Liu Jianjun, chief of the bank's Retail Department, Zhang Jian, chief of Institutional Banking, and deputy heads of a few departments. Ma was in a good mood. He praised me for having the courage and wisdom to abandon investment banking for something meaningful for society. Two years earlier, his bank had launched the "Let a Thousand Wings Fly" program to support small and emerging businesses. Our meeting lasted over one hour, and an elaborate lunch in the boardroom of his Shenzhen head office lasted two hours. At the end of the lunch, Yu and I both felt a bit tired but very encouraged. China Merchants Bank was one of the two banks (the other being Minsheng) that had shown a real commitment to SME lending and consumer finance. If they were to support us, Wansui would be able to expand its lending capabilities enormously.

My third stop was to fly to Beijing to meet Hong Qi, CEO of China Minsheng Bank, arguably the best bank as far as SME lending was concerned. Hong was also my colleague at the People's Bank of China in the 1980s, and we had kept in touch since then. Minsheng had structured its credit function on a sector basis. And it had specialists supporting SME lending in various sectors (catering, textiles, semiconductors, the steel sector, and so on). Some of its branches were dedicated to SME loans. In Guangzhou, for example, my staff had told me that they would often lose customers to Minsheng because the bank was more efficient (in loan decisions) and their terms more attractive due to their lower funding costs.

Minsheng had many efficient regional teams to make SME

loans, and indeed, SME loans had become a major feature of the bank. So Hong did not want to hire outsiders to operate part of the function. That was fair enough.

One of the benefits of my several meetings with Hong and some of the bank's grassroots managers was that I had gained an appreciation on how good their SME operations were. If we could not do business with Minsheng, I figured, at least I could become a shareholder. I soon bought lots of Minsheng's H-shares (1988 HK) listed in Hong Kong. As they say, if you cannot beat them, join them.

Given the bank's rapid growth and the low cost of funding from deposits, I refused to believe that the low valuation of its stock would last very long. I had been a stock analyst at UBS for about eight years, and after being a banker for three years, I had enough confidence in this sector and this bank in particular. In 2011 and 2012, I made a decent profit from this stock. I am still holding some of those shares, and firmly believe that this is a long-term winner.

The other bank I had absolute confidence in was Chongqing Rural Commercial Bank (3618 HK) whose stock was also quoted in the Hong Kong Stock Exchange. In 2012, when I was combing for an investment target from among 60-plus microcredit firms in the Chongqing region, I often came across this bank's credit officers. While I eventually did not find a suitable target to invest in, I fell in love with the bank. The way I see it, microcredit firms are really inferior to well-run banks. Banks have established branch networks and deposit bases. Everyone (existing and prospective customers) has high confidence in them. The cost of switching away from your existing banking relationships is high. In Warren Buffett's words, the banks have a deep and wide "moat." If the banks play their cards properly, they really have mostly prime (good quality) customers who are sticky.

I started to develop an inferiority complex. I began to have doubts about the microcredit sector as a long-term strategy. I bought lots of shares in Chongqing Rural Commercial Bank, and had sat on them despite the unexpected fall from power by Bo Xilai, Chongqing's Communist Party Secretary. When Bo was arrested in the first half of 2012, the stock price of Chongqing Rural Commercial Bank fell more than a third. From my experience, I knew, of course, that Bo was irrelevant to the government-controlled bank. I have held on to the shares and the stock price has recovered. Again, this is one of my long-term holdings. Its valuation was very attractive and business very solid.

I also made pilgrimages and made presentations to smaller banks such as Hangzhou Bank, Ningbo Bank, Guangzhou Agri-Business Bank, Jincheng Bank, and China Resources Bank. None wanted a further discussion on the credit origination agency, because they either had full plates or did not want to take on the risk of having outsiders as their loan originators, whatever the guarantees Wansui's shareholders were willing to provide them.

Some banks had to make politicians happy and wanted to be seen as doing something in SME financing. But they neither had the willingness nor the capability in this area, so they had asked us to sell loan portfolios to them. Since Wansui only had a small loan portfolio of RMB230 million, some banks asked if we could act as an agent to help them source credit portfolios. Then, there came the issue of who would guarantee the full repayment of the loans, and so on. The business model did not seem to work.

Now that China Merchants Bank proved to be the only bank that was willing to explore the credit origination model with Wansui, we started to nail down details.

With blessings from CEO Ma at the head office, we were asked to negotiate details with one of its many branches in Guangzhou. We selected Tianrun Branch. Feng Junxiong, Head of the branch, and Qu Liang, Senior Manager, came to Wansui to conduct due diligence in August 2011. They liked what they had seen and had heard good things about Wansui before. Maybe partly because of the words from the head office, the pair was especially friendly and accommodating. I liked both of them. They were simple and straightforward.

One afternoon, I had a late, long meeting with them in their Guangzhou office and the pair invited me to dinner. I was alone in Guangzhou while my family was in Hong Kong. So, I accepted.

Suddenly I had an idea that these bankers worked like dogs (more so than me in my own days as an investment banker), and hardly had time to eat dinner with their own families. As we arrived at the restaurant, I changed my mind. I insisted on cancelling the dinner. I said to them, "I really want you to go home to eat meals with your families. Please consider this as a brother's goodwill." They did what I said, and were very grateful.

Bankers in China have seen their compensations skyrocket in the past decade but so too has their stress at work. A branch manager like Feng has to meet 20-some KPIs (key performance indicators). For example, they have to meet ever-rising targets on deposits, loans, bad loans, profit margins, as well as benchmarks on fire safety, staff turnover, birth controls, new account openings, and wealth management products, among other things. Apart from facing fierce competition for deposits and for quality borrowers, they have to entertain a long list of people, including corporate customers, and visitors from higher offices, and the government as there are too many government departments.

On one occasion, I learned that Feng was hosting dinners with two groups of visitors at the same time. The two groups were eating dinner in adjacent rooms of the same restaurant. I have learned that this phenomenon was not uncommon among politicians and businessmen.

Friendly and accommodating as they were, when it came to the nitty-gritty details of the credit origination deal, Feng and Qu were every bit as savvy and careful as anyone I had met when I was an investment banker.

Eventually, we came to the conclusion that the process was too onerous for Wansui and its shareholders as the shareholders had to personally guarantee the loans and interest. Moreover, Wansui and its shareholders would also have to buy a loan guarantee (similar to credit default swap) from a reputable agency. Wansui had historically used Yuecai Guarantee Co., an entity owned by the Guangdong Provincial Government. For that guarantee, we would have to pay 3% of the loan balance. This high cost, coupled with the tedious process of due diligence had made the idea of credit origination brokerage unviable. We decided not to proceed in the end.

Contrary to my own frustration, my friends at ZTE Micro Finance, and Zengdai Speed Finance (both based in Shenzhen) successfully convinced the Bank of China and China Construction Bank to accept them as credit origination agents, essentially leveraging off the balance sheets of these banks. Both companies' top managers used to work and received their training at Zhong An Credit in Shenzhen, a pawnshop originally set up by Ping An Insurance Group some 10 years ago. After Ping An went public in the stock exchanges of Shenzhen and Hong Kong some eight or so years earlier, it had sold the tiny pawnshop to Paul Theil in 2006. Theil had been a senior private equity banker at Morgan Stanley in Hong Kong. Before his successful career as an investor, he had been a diplomat at the U.S. Embassy in Beijing in the 1980s. When I was at the Graduate School of the People's Bank of China from 1983 to 1986, Theil was my teacher for one finance course. Theil spoke good Mandarin and was friendly and easygoing. Many of my classmates respected him. Some even ended up working for him at various stages of their careers.

When Liu Jingxiang and Tang Xia, two senior managers at Zhong An Credit left to set up their own shops in 2009 and 2010, Zengdai Real Estate Group and ZTE provided them with funding, respectively. Today, the three companies have become arguably the leaders of the industry. They share some common characteristics. First, each loan they make is small in size (around RMB50,000 each). Second, they each have a large number of branch outlets. For example, ZTE Microcredit has 17 outlets in Shenzhen alone. Third, they all act as banks' credit origination agents as well as lend on their books. And finally they each have a centralized credit assessment system based on IT infrastructure.

At Wansui, we envied them. Our IT system was not up to those standards. As a result, banks had yet to embrace our services.

4
Chapter

Securitization,
Chinese Style

Wansui had a capital base of RMB150 million. With a bank loan equivalent to 50% of our capital, our maximum lending capability was RMB225 million.

That was just not good enough as far as I was concerned. I had plans that needed more of a base than that.

Banks, credit unions, leasing companies, and broker-dealers all have longer leashes on their gearing ratios. More importantly, ordinary industrial companies are subject to no restrictions at all on their gearing ratios. The only constraint they face is lenders' tolerance for risks. I believed that the microcredit industry had been discriminated against. So I led a campaign to challenge the regulations. I made numerous one-on-one personal presentations to officials.

As there had been no national regulation, each province was running its own show. In 2008 when the central bank (People's Bank of China) and bank regulator (China Banking Regulatory Commission) legalized the microcredit industry, it jointly issued a set of guidelines (a regulatory template) and all provinces just copied the template without making many revisions to it. Though many officials had recognized the unfairness of the regulation, every provincial regulator was watching other provinces, and no one wanted to make the first big move in the relaxation of regulations.

However, things were about to change.

In January 2012, the government of Zhejiang Province issued a decree to allow microcredit firms in its jurisdiction to borrow as much as their capital. That was a doubling of the previous permissible leverage. While many observers hailed this relaxation as a breakthrough, it kicked off an ugly turf war. The Zhejiang government clearly had not consulted the banks' regulator (China Banking Regulatory Commission). When one bank after another called its masters in Beijing for the green light, the China Banking Regulatory Commission refused to grant one. Even 18 months later, as this book is going to print, no microcredit firm in Zhejiang has been able to borrow from banks above the previous 50% leverage cap. I made a mental note that the real boss in the industry was still the China Banking Regulatory Commission.

There was another event that taught me the critical importance of the China Banking Regulatory Commission as a spin-off agency from the People's Bank of China. During my honeymoon with the media right after I joined Wansui in June 2011, I received a prominent visitor. Zhang Zi'ai, CEO of China Oriental Asset Management Group, was tall, charming, and soft-spoken. When I first saw him, I thought he looked like Hank Paulson, former United States Treasury Secretary, except that Zhang had silver hair.

Oriental was one of the four entities that the central government created in 2002 to take over nonperforming assets from the four major banks (Industrial and Commercial Bank of China, Agricultural Bank of China, China Construction Bank, and the Bank of China). The other asset management corporations were Cinda, Huarong, and Great Wall. They were similar to the "resolution trusts" of the United States.

Since then, runaway inflation had massively inflated the value of their assets (particularly real estate, factories, toll roads, ports, and mineral assets). Suddenly these four "bad banks" had become valuable commercial entities. Through the sales of their assets, they had gotten billions of yuan in cash, and did not know what to do with the cash. After having splurged on leasing companies, real estate, dealer-brokers and the like, they still had heaps of cash in hand. In order to not compete with banks directly, Oriental had decided to spend some money on microcredit. They thought microcredit was socially desirable and commercially profitable (and safe). Just one week after I joined Wansui, Zhang Zi'ai brought a team of 12 senior managers to visit Wansui. I was very flattered. After listening to my story which they all had read in the papers, and hearing my preliminary thoughts about what Wansui should do going forward, Oriental wanted to explore the possibility of having Wansui manage some of their to-be-created microcredit shops. Their logic was that a state-owned enterprise would be too inefficient for this nitty-gritty operation, and that outsourcing was the only solution. Our answer to their question was a resounding "Yes," of course.

In the months that followed, I led the Wansui team to negotiate with Oriental's senior managers in Guangzhou, Shenzhen, and Beijing on outsourcing. The managers involved on their sides were all very nice, but the matter was an unprecedented one, and no one knew how to overcome the restrictions faced by a commercial entity of the central government.

How would Oriental remunerate Wansui? Easy: fixed commissions, plus performance incentives above a certain profit threshold. It sounded easy, but it was unworkable, because it could encourage Wansui's managers to hide nonperforming and even dead loans. Should Oriental pay Wansui at the end of a 10-year term? Again, Oriental did not want to be tied down for such a long term without the choice of sacking Wansui. They needed more flexibility.

While talking with us, Oriental had tangoed with several other well-regarded microcredit players such as Zengdai and ZTE Microcredit. Nothing had come out of those discussions.

Our many meetings with Oriental had also failed to resolve the hundreds of questions about the process, and in the end Oriental decided to go its own way.

Oriental set up 18 microcredit firms around China, and operated them in-house, having mobilized some of the redundant workforce from its existing business units and hired some extra bodies. Each of these 18 shops was capitalized at between

RMB200 million to RMB300 million.

However, our goodwill with Oriental did produce a tangible benefit for Wansui. In October 2011, just before the bank regulator China Banking Regulatory Commission shut the door on trust companies' dealings with microcredit firms, Oriental signed with Wansui a lending facility amounting to RMB100 million via Xi'An International Trust Company. A trust company was needed to make a loan to Wansui since the loan was not straightforward. It was structured as a securitization deal with Wansui's loan book as collateral. After all, Wansui was not allowed to take a new loan as it had exhausted its leverage limit (the loan limit is set at 50% of Wansui's equity capital). So, for this funding to take place, Wansui must take the securitization route, and Oriental needs the platform of a trust company in order to buy a security.

Any such deal, having obtained the seal of approval from a trust company (which also needs the final approval of the China Banking Regulatory Commission), becomes legal and free of the suspicion of illegal fund-raising.

That was a big vote of confidence in Wansui by a prominent company. Everyone at Wansui appreciated it enormously, as we understood that Zhang Zi'ai had taken some career risks to do this, as the China Banking Regulatory Commission was openly hostile to the microcredit industry. The Commission happened to be the regulator of trust companies and Oriental as well.

As to why the China Banking Regulatory Commission was openly hostile to microcredit firms, there were several explanations, one of which was that the ugly duckling was the brainchild of the central bank (the People's Bank of China), even though the two ministries jointly legalized the microcredit industry in 2008. Given their longstanding rivalry, whatever the People's Bank of China supported, the China Banking Regulatory Commission would dislike and possibly even sabotage. Was this a plausible explanation? I had no way of knowing.

The China Banking Regulatory Commission was not the only entity that was hostile to microcredit. Other government departments and the public held a negative view too. Even the provincial or city regulators of the industry (the Finance Department) mostly looked down upon the industry as something sneaky, dodgy, destructive to moral standards, and harmful to the overall stability of the financial industry.

In November 2011, the China Banking Regulatory Commission issued a decree to all banks, preventing trust companies from raising funds for microcredit companies. My securitization plan seemed dead in the water. I did not want to rely too much on just one trust company (Xi'An International Trust Company), so I approached China Resources Trust which was headquartered in Shenzhen.

There were very nice working-level people and one of them, Yuan Wu, used to work with me at UBS, and we had got on well. Her team leader, Liu Qian, 31, had been a prolific dealmaker. They had wanted to find a smart way to raise funds for microcredit companies without violating the China Banking Regulatory Commission's ban.

In the first four months of 2012, we had many conference calls and meetings with the team at China Resources Trust but they did not feel comfortable about our game-plans. Liu escalated our deal to his CEO, Meng Yang, and her deputy, Lu Qiang. Lu was one of the luminaries who had visited Wansui in the first few weeks of my work at Wansui. He thought our SME lending business was socially desirable, our team professional, and our safety better than run-of-the-mill microlenders. However, we knew that we had to play safe on the regulatory front. A solution was for Lu to call on the head of the China Banking Regulatory Commission's Non-Bank Regulation Department for "an understanding" while I was to go and visit Shang Fulin, the chairman of the Commission, to get his support. After all, what we were trying to accomplish was really to increase our capability to lend to SMEs, a group that the central government had always wanted banks to support.

Shang had just come to head the China Banking Regulatory Commission, having spent eight years as Chairman of the China Securities Regulatory Commission. I used to work for Shang at the central bank in 1986 to 1989. At the time, he was the People's Bank of China's Head of the Interest Rate Division, I was a principal staff member at the Reform Division, and we sat in the same small office, desk-to-desk.

I had always admired Shang for his hunger and ability to learn new things. From 1986 to 1987, for example, he was one of the very few central bankers to learn how to use a mainframe computer system at the central bank, and one of the few to thoroughly understand the internal statistics system in the banking industry. He had learned all this in his free time, such as on lunch breaks or tea breaks, while most of us lazybones played cards, took naps, or played ping pong. In his forties, he still went on to earn a PhD in economics through a part-time program.

People who have worked with Shang in the past few decades all privately agree that he has a reputation for being rigorous, diligent, and squeaky clean. He rarely makes off-the-cuff comments on policy issues. He commands wide respect.

I do not blame the China Banking Regulatory Commission for the discrimination against the microcredit industry. Many other departments are just as negative. So is the public. Even the local regulator of the microcredit industry does not trust its subjects.

Clearly, the whole nation has to come to terms with equal access to finance as only then can the country's struggling SMEs and underprivileged consumers no longer be haunted by the long-lasting damage of the current regulations.

This is just like the gun control issue in the United States, or the protection of the environment in China: no one great man or great entity can force the necessary changes. It will require national consensus.

> **// Clearly, the whole nation has to come to terms with equal access to finance as only then can the country's struggling SMEs and underprivileged consumers no longer be haunted by the long-lasting damage of the current regulations. //**

Anyone can see the logic behind gun control and background checks in the United States, or a substantial rise in water tariffs or gas charges in China, and yet no politician has the guts, or power, to get it done.

As to China's microcredit industry, only when a national consensus is reached can we have a sensible and conducive regulatory environment.

At our meeting, Shang explained to me that he was not up to speed with the microcredit industry, having just moved over from the China Securities Regulatory Commission. However, he knew that hidden risks existed because some microcredit players made loans and raised finances parallel to their licensed microcredit firms. In other words, some licensed microcredit companies were just fronts for much bigger but unreported financing activities. I had not known this, and briefed him about what we were doing at Wansui, and what I wanted to achieve. I assured him that Wansui would only do the right thing, and that most other microcredit companies were in full compliance with regulations, though the regulations were stifling, in my view.

Sadly, neither I nor Lu of China Resources Trust had secured any assurance from our visits that the China Banking Regulatory Commission was about to loosen its ban on trust companies' fundraising for microcredit firms. We had decided to wait until such a relaxation became a reality. More than one year on, the China Banking Regulatory Commission seemed to harden its stance.

Now it became clear that three of the things I wanted to do were in trouble.

First, the government was unlikely to allow Wansui and others to borrow beyond 50% of our capital.

Second, trust companies would not be allowed to raise funds for us. Securitization of loans had become just a pipe dream. Third, while we managed to get one contract management deal in Changde, the second such deal had proven elusive. Oriental, potentially the biggest catch, was going its own way.

Luckily for me and Wansui, I had come up with a backup plan a few months earlier.

Just three months after I left UBS to join Wansui, a small Hong Kong-listed company, Man Sang International Limited (0938 HK), approached me to become its CEO, and tie their future to the tantalizing microcredit sector in China. I signed up.

Now I was wearing two hats, and my plan was for Man Sang to acquire control over Wansui and other better-run rivals elsewhere in China.

5
Chapter

Regulatory Nightmares

No one ever enjoys dealing with regulators, especially Chinese regulators. The necessary evil gets worse when a cross-border transfer of funds is involved.

I should have known this, as I had been a senior banker at UBS for three years, and before that a research analyst on Chinese equities. When I was running Shenzhen Investment Limited from 2006 to 2008, I had encountered few hurdles in getting cross-border deals done.

So I thought that I could navigate a merger between Man Sang and Wansui, as well as other players later on. But this turned out to be a nightmare.

Two decades ago, Man Sang started to manufacture and process jewels for the European market on an OEM basis (contract manufacturing). In 1997, it became big enough and got listed on the Hong Kong Stock Exchange. In the past 10 years or so, it had not grown as competition became fiercer. Its chairman and controlling shareholder, Ricky Cheng, was also chairman of China South City, another company listed in Hong Kong. I could see that Cheng's full energy had turned towards property development, a more profitable and scalable business than jewel manufacturing.

Cheng was one of my clients when I was an investment banker at UBS. My team had sold a corporate bond for his property business in early 2011. A couple of years earlier, Cheng and I had chatted about transforming Man Sang into something else given its lack of growth prospects.

When I left UBS for Wansui, Cheng was rather curious. At a dinner several weeks later, he asked what microcredit was all about and how it was regulated. We quickly agreed that we should probably do something together. I had known Cheng for three years and had always liked his shrewdness, motivation, and sense of humor. On September 20, 2011, three months after I had become Chairman of Wansui, I took on an extra job as CEO at

Man Sang. We announced that we wanted to transform Man Sang into a growing player in the microcredit space.

VIE: Small Tricks

Immediately, Man Sang dispatched a due diligence team to Wansui. That was straightforward. Due to my double roles, I had stayed largely detached, and allowed the lawyers, auditors, and other managers on both sides to dig, enquire, respond, and negotiate.

When it came to the restructuring of an acquisition deal, the headaches started. The regulations in Guangdong and most other provinces specifically prevent a foreign entity from investing in, let alone controlling, a microcredit firm.

That's fine. To bypass the regulation, we would adopt a structure under which Man Sang would become the manager of Wansui indefinitely for a service fee each year. Lawyers call it a VIE (variable interest entities) structure. Many deals had been done that way in the so-called strategically-important sectors where regulation prevented a foreign party from taking a controlling interest in a domestic firm. But in those deals I had seen, one thing was common: The shareholders of the foreign entity and of the domestic entity were essentially the same group of people. In other words, the same bunch of people signed away the management rights of the domestic business to themselves.

But in the case of Man Sang and Wansui, the shareholders were not the same group of people. In addition, inefficient rules in Guangdong do not allow the existence of a controlling shareholder in a microcredit firm, and require a diverse shareholding structure.

After spending hundreds of thousands of dollars on lawyers, auditors, and bankers, wasting a few months talking to the 12 shareholders of Wansui on the tedious terms of the VIE agreements, both Cheng and I had had enough. We let the negotiations drift while checking on other acquisition targets. Chongqing in central China was an obvious target.

The Fatal Attraction of Chongqing

Chongqing is located in central China, along the Yangtze River. Income per head there was probably half of Guangdong's. But its economy was booming, and the government there was eager to catch up with the coastal provinces. A couple of weeks after I joined Wansui, Luo Guang, Head of Chongqing Government's Finance Department reached out to me. He not only called to congratulate me, but also requested a meeting. He and Yuan Wei, a divisional chief of his department, flew to Guangzhou to meet me in late July 2011.

Their plane was delayed (flight delays had become very common in recent years), and when they eventually landed in Guangzhou, their taxi driver got totally lost in the re-routing of roads, and was then caught in a traffic jam. They were three hours late for our scheduled meeting.

We met at the lobby bar of the Westin Hotel, near the Guangzhou East Rail Station. Luo apologized profusely. He was my age (48), and slightly overweight. He radiated energy, and enthusiasm. He gave me a full-blown presentation on the microcredit industry in Chongqing, the refreshingly simple regulations, and generous tax concessions. I must say he was very different from the mainstream officials we knew, and I liked him.

"Wait no longer. Come and set up a microcredit firm in Chongqing. I will guarantee that red tape will not get in your way. The shortage of capital in Chongqing will give you lots of business." Luo concluded his presentation, asking when I would make a visit to Chongqing. I was impressed.

It was six in the evening, and I asked him to stay for dinner. No. He had to take the evening flight back to Chongqing, as there were too many other things to attend to the next day. So, I ordered a good bottle of wine for the three of us.

Luo lived up to his promise. When I eventually started to explore acquisitions in Chongqing, he and his office did lend a helping hand, for which we were very appreciative. However, the local branch of the People's Bank of China, the central bank, became a major hurdle. The China Banking Regulatory Commission and the regulators of the capital markets and insurance industry were central government functions, a bit like the United States Federal system. So local and regional governments had limited influence on them. Luo helped me get clearance very quickly from the city's Foreign Investment Department. When I met with resistance from the People's Bank of China in Chongqing, Luo called several meetings to mediate. But eventually the intransigence of the People's Bank of China prevailed.

Until this day, I still do not fully understand what the People's Bank of China's objection was all about. In 2011, the People's Bank of China created a new department called the Cross-Border Renminbi Regulation Department. The idea of this department was to channel the massive amounts of renminbi in Hong Kong and elsewhere back into China in an orderly manner. But vague rules and arbitrary implementation drove businessmen crazy. I was told that the application Man Sang lodged to set up a holding company was wrong, as the Bank had just introduced a new set of rules. I spent a week in Chongqing trying to find a solution but to no avail.

In late 2012, Luo was transferred to another government job, as the Chairman of Southwest Securities, a mid-size investment bank. I discussed with Luo the possibility of Southwest acquiring a small broker-dealer in Hong Kong, but he was suddenly sacked. Sadly, he was implicated in the famous sex scandal that rocked Chongqing, and it brought down about 10 government officials. A young woman slept with these officials but secretly filmed the act. She used these pictures to blackmail the officials and this eventually led to their sackings. I felt sorry for Luo, a capable man with drive and enthusiasm. I hope he gets his feet on the ground again.

Car Accident in Chongqing

Having made four trips to Chongqing without achieving anything, I became frustrated. I sent Jiang, Wansui's Chief Operating officer, to try her luck. She had some friends in high places there. But she wasted even more time there without achieving a solution. One day, I got a call from a panicked Wilson Cheng, my assistant at Man Sang, who was in Chongqing that week helping Jiang with the registration of a new holding company. Jiang had been hit in a traffic accident and been taken to the hospital. A truck had hit Jiang's taxi at a road junction. Her head and back were injured, though Cheng was not hurt.

The second day, I flew to Chongqing to see Jiang. She looked pale, and was still in shock. After trying three hospitals the previous night in vain, she had eventually gotten a room after a senior government official intervened. She stayed at the hospital for about 10 days, and then flew to Guangzhou to continue her recovery. It took her another month to walk properly.

Starting to Lose Heart

Jiang's accident was the final straw. I had come to the view that even Chongqing, where officials were more sympathetic to the struggle of businessmen, was like this! I was not willing to waste more time racing through the regulatory mazes. In February 2012, as a shareholder and advisor of another finance group, China Finance International Investment (0721 HK) whose stock is also listed in Hong Kong, I had gone with its CEO, Liu Baorui, to meet regulatory officials in Tianjin, another city that was said to be more proactive in attracting outside investments into the microcredit and private equity sectors.

I ended up being totally discouraged. The extensive wining-and-dining and back-scratching were off-putting to me. The rules were just as hard as in other provinces. Other people were willing to put up with those things, but not me.

Doing business is hard enough. Serving customers, marketing, and financing are what I wanted to spend more time on. But spending month after month on corporate registration alone was a terrible way to allocate your resources. Maybe the microcredit industry was the wrong sector to tackle?

Running Other People's Businesses

In late 2011, before we had failed to register a holding company in Chongqing, I got Wansui people to explore more contract management deals. At the time, the government had just approved the creation of 10 microcredit firms in Guangzhou city proper.

In my view, to succeed, a microcredit firm must be near its customers who are usually the owners of restaurants, teahouses, florists, groceries, and furniture stores. But politicians do not want to understand business and are more interested in putting on nice shows. So, they forced these 10 microcredit firms to rent offices in the same street (Changdi) and even in the same building. Clearly the location was not convenient for customers.

Officials call the street "Microcredit Street." There is a rumor that some officials might have ownership stakes in the building, and thus have a vested interest to support the rentals, but that has not been substantiated.

As the 10 microcredit firms opened their doors, I saw an opportunity for Wansui to export our management expertise. Indeed, Yuexiu Microcredit, a government outfit, came to Wansui for help. From 2007 to 2008, I was a non-executive board director of Yuexiu's parent company, a real estate developer. I wanted to accept their invitation to manage their shop, but Jiang was strongly against the idea. Her reasoning was that contract management within the same city would be similar to helping a competitor. After all, Wansui would eventually expand into the city proper from our current base in the suburban Huadu District. That sounded right, but I disagreed. Even if Wansui did not accept the assignment, someone else might. There were many well-managed players around. After all, running a microcredit shop was not rocket science.

As I was spending more time with Man Sang in Hong Kong, Jiang had effectively become the boss of Wansui, as all employees were recruited by her. I noticed in my first month at Wansui, that she had an overbearing personality. Other managers either had loyalty to Jiang, or felt caught between the crossfire of the two strong personalities of Jiang and myself.

Power Struggle at Wansui

Despite my urging, Jiang blocked my idea of managing the operation for Yuexiu Microcredit. Sure enough, Yuexiu soon hired its own employees and got the ball off the ground.

A few weeks earlier, Jiang also killed my suggestion of exploring the agency business of raising funds for corporate customers when Wansui did not have the money or willingness to lend to them. In essence, this was merchant banking. A lot of boutique shops had sprung up in recent years to serve this nice niche. One such shop, Noah Holdings Limited, even got listed in the NASDAQ Capital Markets.

I was upset at these two episodes, and called Jiang to announce that she was no longer Chief Operating Officer at Wansui. She was still an employee, and a shareholder. Wansui would continue to pay her a salary and pick up her medical bills. She could still use a company car with a paid chauffer. She would be free to come back to work once she fully recovered. In March 2012, she left Wansui while remaining a shareholder.

6
Chapter

Peer-to-Peer (P2P) Banking

In April 2012, I resigned from my CEO position at Man Sang and this marked the end of my wasteful pursuit of the microcredit sector through a Hong Kong-listed company and foreign funds. I had a three-year contract and drew an annual salary of at least HKD5 million, and I believe I was overpaid. In February 2012, I asked the Board of Directors to cut my base salary in half and I took full responsibility for the slow progress of the business. Chairman Cheng appreciated my candid assessment of the weak performance, but suggested that I keep the base salary unchanged.

I was under a lot of pressure to boost the team's performance.

We labored on for another two months. I saw no progress. After Jiang's traffic accident in Chongqing, and the incidents which lead to her sacking, I had decided that I had to acknowledge reality: my efforts to turn Man Sang into a microcredit player were not going to work and so I had to resign immediately.

Chairman Cheng was a generous friend, and it was not easy for me to leave his company. We talked three times and in the end he accepted my resignation. It was an unpleasant ending. But it was the best possible outcome at that juncture.

Looking back now, I see that at Wansui it had taken me quite a while to figure out two key operational issues. Once I figured them out, I pushed reforms through.

The first issue was how to organize the frontline staff.

Before I arrived at Wansui, the team was organized so that everyone had to become an "all around generalist." The same employee would have to distribute pamphlets, make cold calls, visit borrowers to verify the information that they had provided, and collect money at maturity.

Jiang was a strong supporter of this model but I discovered that this model was too demanding for our young recruits.

Some people are just not good at certain things. If you push them too hard, they will get demoralized and quit. Once they quit, you leave some customers unattended. Once some high achievers quit for other reasons, the management team will freak out because those high achievers had become irreplaceable.

Of course, when an outstanding customer manager owns a big number of good customers, they can start to demand things and the firm's compensation structure will start to shake.

Finally, there is the bottleneck.

Realistically, the maximum number of customers that a customer manager can handle is always limited in any given month to, let's say, 50 or 70 customers.

One of our young ladies who was exceptionally competent handled 200 customers in a month. When she got married in February 2012, she went to work in her husband's city in Jiangxi Province and I almost cried when she left!

So, I decided to implement a new system more commonly seen in other firms. We would split our frontline team into three teams: marketing, assessment, and collection. And the loan approval team headed by the Chief Risk Officer had always been separate. So, we improved the scalability of our business model and did not have to work until late in the evening every night.

Making this transition took a few months, but the pain was worth it. Yu deserved a lot of credit.

The second issue where I changed things was when I got Wansui to stop making bridge loans. Almost all microcredit firms in China make bridge loans. In the Chinese banking system, when a bank loan matures on, say, Wednesday, the borrower must repay the loan before the bank can approve a new loan three or five days later. This rule is probably unique to China, and is designed to ensure that bank managers do not renew loans automatically to hide non-performing loans. As Chinese banks make a growing number of short-term loans, the renewal of loans becomes a big phenomenon.

The system is a bit absurd too.

How can an ongoing business suddenly stop operation and hand the money to the bank, and get a new loan three days later? This puts a lot of pressure on any borrower to maintain high cash flows and multiple banking relationships.

There's nothing wrong with that rule, but following it comes at a price, literally. Grassroots bank managers worked out a clever solution.

Enter the microcredit firms and unlicensed money lenders (which ironically are sometimes funded by banks). They lend to the borrowers for three days and charge, say, 1% to 2%! If you annualize that interest rate, that's extremely high. Some operators thrive on this line of business. As long as you have a few contacts inside a bank, you will be regularly fed this type of opportunity.

There's nothing illegal or wrong here. But as I see it, the bank manager probably fools his superiors about the dependable cash flows of the borrower. Everyone lives under the false comfort of dealing with quality customers.

At times, this can get tricky. After the bank gets the loan back from the borrower thanks to the bridge loan from a microcredit firm, the central government, or the upper echelon of the bank, suddenly tightens the lending quotas for that region or the whole country (it happens often), and the branch-level bank manager suddenly finds that he actually does not have the latitude to make a new loan to the borrower, as he has verbally promised.

Now the microcredit firm has become the victim of the sudden jolt. The microcredit firm may not even hold collateral, as the borrower's limited amount of collateral has been pledged to the bank. As most companies operate with a high leverage, they simply do not have enough collateral to go around.

"Just three days. Our new loan has been approved by the bank in principle." That is the assurance I often hear.

But more than just a few microcredit firms have been left holding the bag.

Of course, the borrower cannot afford to pay this type of high interest rate for a long time. A dispute with the microcredit firm may start to escalate. And an overdue loan may eventually become a dead loan.

Even six months after my arrival, Wansui was still a modest player in this business segment, though it had never been jolted by a bank's sudden change of mind.

I was never comfortable about the risks associated with this business. I raised objections. But the team wanted to continue to offer that product. I had to make a tough decision to stop it knowing it was a lucrative practice. I thought that the risk-reward balance did not justify the continuation of it. If things went smoothly, you got 1% to 2%. But if things went sour, you lost 100%. That's a lousy gamble.

I wrote an article about my reasoning for the objection and my decision to cut that product offering. After the piece was posted on my blog as well as the Wansui website, lots of people in the industry reacted positively to it.

Some wiser players never even contemplated that product in the first place.

Admitting Defeat

In Eastern as well as Western culture, we are all taught to persevere, and never give up. Failure carries a big stigma. As a Chinese man who has received much of my education in the West, and worked almost two decades at Western institutions, I consider myself neither Chinese nor Western. At school and in the workplace in Beijing, Hong Kong, and Canberra, I have sometimes found myself a loner. Though I'd like to consider myself open-minded and easygoing, I do not always conform to mainstream expectations.

If I found myself in a cocktail party (there were only four such occasions so far), I would feel a bit lonely and would find an excuse to escape. So far, I have only attended four or five wedding banquets while my own marriage took place at City Hall in Hong Kong.

When I have left a workplace (which I have done about 10 times so far, including three times at UBS), I would never send a farewell message to colleagues, long or short.

Lots of people talk up the importance of networking. But I generally pay little attention. I have yet to sign up with Facebook or Twitter; Keeping track of 3,000 friends on Facebook seems to mean nothing to me as I am already overwhelmed by things to do in the real world.

To be sure, I am not anti-social. I run a reasonably active blog in Chinese. I publish my analysis and opinions regularly on current affairs, economic policy, microcredit matters, and the capital markets.

Since 2008, my blog has received 6 million hits, and my articles have often been reprinted by newspapers and websites. I run a small charity program, having donated almost RMB600,000 to Maliang High School which I graduated from, and the Guangdong Charity Foundation where Wansui is located. The funding all came from the royalties of my two Chinese books and public speeches.

A New Chapter for Wansui

Having quit Man Sang, I focused my energies on Wansui. There were so many things I had to attend to: IT needs, staff training, and filling accounting loopholes, among other things. While these are by no means easy tasks, they are more enjoyable to me than dealing with regulators.

I must confess we made virtually no progress on IT infrastructure. Being entirely non-tech savvy, I felt helpless. I gave the task to Yu and Wang Lixin, the CFO. They proved to be not much better at it. I came to realize that the IT business was more than just software and hardware. Successful deployment of an IT infrastructure is an electronic reflection on the management process. We invited Kingdee and a few other software companies to Wansui to brainstorm, and we also visited some IT-savvy microcredit companies. Hopefully, one day Wansui will sort out its IT issues.

An Expansion Strategy

After August 2011, I got Wansui to experiment with an expansion strategy in partnership with some friendly companies that had an extensive branch network not only in Guangdong, but also in other provinces. However, we failed to get a deal off the ground. It's worth noting that, until this day, no other microcredit firm seems to have succeeded on this front. I wonder if our business logic was wrong.

My logic was as follows: For microcredit firms to succeed, you either have to have an internet strategy, or an army of low-cost "foot soldiers." Since I do not know anything about the internet (or IT infrastructure), and Wansui is an old school operator, I decided to lay out a low-cost network or, to be precise, take a ride on other people's low-cost networks.

I identified two types of potential partners: one was the real estate agencies or insurance brokers with thousands of outlets.

The other was the fertilizer distributors with retail networks.

Right after Wansui's management team agreed on this strategy, we hit the road. The first company we visited was Hopefluent Group Holdings (0733 HK), whose stock had been listed on the Hong Kong Stock Exchange. I had met chairman Fu and his son before. We had a good meeting with the father and son, but they already had a plan to experiment with the idea on its own.

We then visited an insurance broker, CNinsure (NASDAQ: CISG), whose shares were listed on the NASDAQ stock market. CNinsure had already rolled out a microcredit business with the acquisition of some licenses across China. This line of business fit nicely with their mortgage-brokerage business. They also wanted to go their own way.

We then turned to the fertilizer distribution company, Sinofert (0297 HK), a Hong Kong-listed company. Through the introduction of its top management in Beijing, we met the senior managers of its Guangdong Division. They did not seem interested in tedious work. It was a government-controlled operation. I can understand their lack of enthusiasm.

We decided to try Guangdong Tianhe Agricultural Company, under the provincial government's Supply-Sales Cooperative Network. This cooperative was a Communist era relic. In most provinces and cities, this entity had disappeared into the dust, but in Guangdong, it has survived, largely due to a more pragmatic leader in Li Chaoming. Incidentally, Li and I went to university together in Wuhan from 1979 to 1983, and we got on well.

Our initial negotiations with Tianhe were very smooth. After some nice meals and candid discussions on business principles and operational issues, we quickly got down to the specific terms of the joint venture. Wansui wanted to deploy only two to three credit marketing people in some of their vast retail networks.

Wansui does not have to pay rentals or obtain permissions to open branches. I figured that those who buy fertilizers, seed, and pesticides are also likely to need microcredit. Our logic was sound, or so it seemed.

Tianhe conducted due diligence on Wansui and was happy with the result. However, Tianhe went quiet for weeks despite my several telephone calls. Later on, it emerged that Tianhe did not want to set up a joint venture because it had just lodged its application with the securities watchdog to go public on the domestic stock market. Under the Chinese regulations, an IPO applicant must not experience any operational, ownership, or management change in the two years leading up to its IPO. Not even the slightest bit of a change! Any such change could be used as an excuse by the securities officials to shoot down your IPO application. Stability is the key. Effectively, this means that an IPO applicant must hold its breath and avoid anything that will complicate its IPO.

This is ridiculous! Having worked for so many years at investment banks, I know how important an IPO is for a Chinese company. In the domestic stock market, valuation is sky high, and hundreds of IPO aspirants focus on the IPO and allow everything else to take a backseat.

When there are hundreds of millions in free money up for grabs, who can blame the companies concerned for shortsightedness or a sudden change of mind?

With several hundred outlets in Guangdong serving the farmers, Tianhe was a perfect fit for Wansui. But we had to understand Tianhe's preoccupation with the IPO.

Almost 18 months later, Tianhe was still anxiously waiting for the China Securities Regulatory Commission's green-light for its IPO. And it does not even know how much longer it will have to wait, as the Commission had stopped all IPOs in October

2012. According to the government, there are still close to 700 companies waiting in the wings, after over 100 companies have thrown in the towel since the fall of 2012.

More Fundraising at Wansui

As of early 2012, we tried another route to raise funds. Ping An Group, the second biggest insurance company in China with a bank and trust company attached, had just set up an online fund-raising platform for the microcredit industry named the Lujiazui Finance Exchange. After extensive due diligence, they accepted Wansui as their very first user. We put an RMB10 million loan parcel on the Ping An exchange, which in turn sold the parcel at RMB50,000 a unit to its employees. Wansui paid an 11% annualized rate, while investors received 8% on an annualized basis. The 3% difference was the gross fees for the Ping An exchange.

This was only a test run. Later on, Ping An broadened its reach to investors beyond its employees. There was always the regulatory concern: did the exchange have a license for banking business? Was this similar to the peer-to-peer funding model?

In June 2012, Gregory Gibb, the head of the Ping An exchange and the Chief Innovation Officer at Ping An Group, who used to work at McKinsey & Company and more recently at a Taiwan bank, took me to see Ma Mingzhe, his chairman, probably hoping that I could convince Ma to allow the Ping An exchange to support microcredit in general and Wansui in particular. But most of the one-hour meeting was for Ma to complain about the bad behavior in the microcredit industry and the downside risks for the Ping An exchange. He had even quoted his candid chats with one of his friends who happened to run such a business.

Confused and frustrated, I asked why Ma was so negative

on the sector. Ma replied that he was deeply worried about the very high interest rates some microcredit firms charge customers. Those rates were well above the regulatory ceiling of 24% annual rates, according to his friend. Ma believed that this type of violation of regulation was not an isolated incidence. This, continued Ma, would sooner or later push large numbers of borrowers over the edge and spark a subprime credit crisis. A regulatory clampdown would not be too far away, if that were to occur, he argued.

I was surprised he did not want to hear my full story. Maybe he did, but I was not convincing enough. His mind had been made up, and his views were strong.

What I did not understand is why his insurance arm ran a successful and sizable (probably the biggest in China) microcredit business, albeit through the selling of credit guarantees.

Before I had met Ma, Gibb also arranged for me to meet another heavyweight, Gu Min, the executive director of Ping An Group, and Gibb's alumni at McKinsey. Gu was fast-talking and sharp. We had a quick lunch together, and he urged me to see Ma. Maybe he had known of Ma's negative stance?

I learned later on that the Ping An exchange had stopped buying microcredit loan portfolios to on-sell to retail investors online. It had turned itself into an online matching service for small

> **//** For the subprime credit market to prosper, there is a genuine need for multiple providers of information and analysis. **//**

borrowers and retail lenders, similar to other online operators such as renrendai.com. The Ping An exchange is now getting into credit rating services for consumers and businesses, an exclusive confine of the central bank thus far. Given the political clout and market influence of Ping An Group, I am sure they will succeed.

For the subprime credit market to prosper, there is a genuine need for multiple providers of information and analysis. I think Ping An is well positioned to fill that need. I have found Gibb and his team, including Huang Liming, very experienced and high-caliber professionals. In mid-2012, Ping An and Wansui even contemplated a joint venture rating agency just for the microcredit sector (at least initially), but the economics did not seem to justify the venture, and we had to drop the idea.

Online Microcredit Operators

Well before I joined Wansui, I had started to pay attention to peer-to-peer (P2P) credit operators, the most prominent of which is CreditEase founded by Tang Ning, who received his education in China and later in the U.S. His firm employs tens of thousands of people in probably over 100 cities. It does not have a license as a financial institution. To avoid being shut down by the government, CreditEase has taken full advantage of the law that allows individuals (as opposed to a company) to lend to anyone. At CreditEase, all lending is done in the name of Tang Ning personally, and all creditors lend to Tang personally. To scale up, Tang securitizes his loan portfolios to retail investors with the assistance of trust companies and third-party wealth management companies such as Noah Private Wealth Management. CreditEase has started to utilize electronic means to acquire customers and investors, but it mainly relies on foot soldiers. In 2011 and 2012, I ran into Tang at almost all seminars and forums as he works very hard to disseminate his message of helping the little guys.

In 2011 and 2012, I spent a fair amount of time with

Hangzhou-based 6677bank.com, but sadly it went belly up in early 2013, having burned through all of its cash in three years. In early 2012, it had a staff of 300. Its business model was to attract borrowers through its website, and upon preliminary assessment, it would refer qualified applicants to one of its partner banks, instead of matching them with online investors. I think the biggest factor behind its downfall was that it was unable to attract enough acceptable borrowers online. As a result, banks have found 6677bank.com a Mickey Mouse player, and not at all dependable. This has led to a vicious cycle. If applicants fail to have their loan demands met often enough, their interest in the website also declines. This downward spiral can continue until the company flames out. In its three-year lifespan, advertising had proven to be very essential and very expensive.

Major online P2P operators include renrendai.com and ppdai.com. Unlike 6677bank.com, these two operators match loan applicants with retail investors. I met them, but I have so far not analyzed them carefully enough. I am skeptical about the viability of their business model, even if they never face a regulatory risk. The reason is because the investors do not get a chance to meet the borrowers, and no one stands to guarantee the safety of their money. From my own experience at Wansui and two other players I invested in, I know how big a leap of faith is required. Even if they prosper for some time, these firms are vulnerable to a scandal, or a fraud on the part of borrowers. Partly as a result of this fear, Hongling Chuangtou (www.my089.com), a prudent operator in Shenzhen, conducts due diligence on borrowers, and guarantees the safety of its investors' money. In a sense, the website is only a marketing tool. For due diligence to work in a cost-effective way, it has limited its operations to Shenzhen.

Farewell to Wansui, Sort of

In July 2012, the biggest shareholder (with 60% of the shares through various names and accounts) of Wansui sold its stake to Huayin, a metal trader in Foshan. I remain the second biggest shareholder with a 10% stake. Huayin wanted to run the operation, and I had to take a backseat. I resigned as chairman, but remain a director and shareholder. I handed day-to-day operational responsibility to Huayin soon after that.

Ironically, to officially change the chairmanship requires a lengthy process. When this book goes to print in mid-2013, I will still be listed as Chairman on the regulator's website, and I am still Chairman as far as they are concerned. I am a 10% shareholder of Wansui and it will require a huge amount of paperwork to have that reflected in the government's files and corporate registry.

7

Chapter

Moonlighting Banks and Bankers

One of the small benefits of being a celebrity is that lots of people call you to bounce around business ideas. Sometimes you are asked to partner with them. If nothing else, this can stimulate your thinking.

But it can also distract you.

Since 2011, I have been invited to give numerous paid speeches in China, Hong Kong, and Singapore. In most cases, the subject is either microcredit or the stock market. One businessman in Yangzhou, Jiangsu Province, invited me to be a ceremonial — though paid — chairman of his microcredit company to facilitate his application for a license.

High Cost Lending as PE Deals

After I left Man Sang in April 2012 to focus on Wansui, a small private equity guy named Deng Jinyong called me after a common friend in real estate connected us.

Deng wanted to meet to discuss a private equity idea.

So he came to Wansui's office in Guangzhou with a beautiful young assistant, Jenny Yong, a fresh graduate from local Jinan University. I learned later on that Yong's father was the Chief of the Propaganda Department in a Provincial Communist Party, and a hotshot in line for a more senior post in Beijing. She had interned at HSBC in Shanghai a year earlier.

Deng, about 50, used to run a Chinese TV maker's export business in Egypt in the 1990s. Prior to that, he also spent some years working for an American electronics company in California. When we met, he had recently befriended Wang Tian, a cousin of the president of a Chinese bank. The bank had a list of 15 approved private equity firms to work with. His one-man shop — well, one man plus an assistant, to be precise — Ever Prosper, had been selected as one of 15 such lucky firms. Deng said that that status was an enormous privilege and an effortless way to make lots of money.

"How do you plan to work with the big bank?" I was curious.

"Easy. As long as we find a plausible investment project, we will get the bank to raise money for us. We will have a virtually unlimited amount of money to invest. You know the banks all have a fund pool." Deng was excited.

"You mean the bank will sell a so-called wealth management product to the public, just like any other fundraising for private equity firms?"

"Exactly. But we are one of the Lucky 15. We are not just another PE firm. Even KKR, Carlyle, or TPG, or the domestic firms such as Jiuding Capital, does not have that privilege." He boasted.

"But you do not seem to have any investing or banking experience. Why will the bank trust you?" I probed.

"That is why I am here to see you. You are well-known and quoted in the papers every day. A few weeks ago, I drank Maotai with some bigwigs at the bank's head office, and they said they had gone to college with you in the 1980s."Deng almost shouted, with his hands waving in the air.

"How do you want me to help you?" I was interested.

"Simple. Join my partnership. Take a 20% equity stake. I will keep 50% as I have given a 30% stake to the bank president's cousin. But do not tell anyone about this 30% stake," Deng whispered.

Aha! I got it.

No. I cannot associate myself with this sort of thing. I said to myself. Deng thought I wanted a bigger stake, and explained that my stake was for free. He said that he had spent 40 million Renminbi on office costs and gifts for the relevant bankers who were to select the Lucky 15.

I was not even slightly interested. To me, this was hair-raising stuff. Deng's assistant Yong took out a sleek presentation pack with pictures and descriptions of some investment projects.

I asked Deng another question, "You have the Lucky 15 status, and investment targets have been lined up. Why do you want me to join you?"

"I only have the Lucky 15 status in two provinces: Hubei and Guangdong. That means that I can only raise funds and invest in these two places with money raised by the bank. It would be nice to upgrade it to a national status. Besides, this status is subject to annual reviews. With you as a partner or even a chairman, we should get through the annual reviews more easily. After all, we have to hire a bunch of young bankers to work on the projects, and you need to teach them how to crunch numbers, and guide them on writing PowerPoint presentations. I do not know that stuff. But I am good at hanging around with the big guys, drinking, golfing, and tipping them," Deng explained.

I flipped through Deng's presentation pack. There was a wastewater treatment plant and a biodegradable plastics company in Wuhan, and a scrap metal trader and a city rail project in Guangdong. While some of these projects were probably sensible and viable, they were either too small, or too unattractive for the IPO market. Indeed, when I was a banker I had visited the scrap metal company in Guangdong. It was not big enough to go public, even in three years' time.

If they cannot do an IPO in two or three years, how are the PE investors going to exit the deals? After all, there is always a long queue of companies to go public, and the Chinese securities regulator sometimes closes the door on IPOs, as it did in October 2012, leaving 800 or so IPO aspirants out in the cold. It also stopped all IPOs in 2003 to 2004 as the stock market was sluggish.

Clearly, Deng knew the ropes. "Easy. Some of these projects are currently owned by city governments. We will invest, say, 20% to 35% equity in them. But we will sign with them a buyback clause, guaranteed by their fiscal revenue or cash flows somewhere. We know some of them are not IPO material, but who cares? Our investment is just a loan when things do not pan out."

"Why do you not call it a loan?"

"You fool! Government-controlled banks are not allowed to lend at 20% or 25% internal rate of returns. You know the prime lending rate is only 6% these days. Second, the banks are subject to lending quotas each year. No matter how many deposits the banks may have, they must work within a lending limit. The limit is not only applicable to each bank as a whole, but also its regional branches. Finally, there is the 75% loan-to-deposit ratio banks have to comply with. Sometimes, the limit is lower, maybe 70%, whatever. The banks' top brass want to be seen as having a lower ratio, you know. It just looks better."

I continued to probe, "Deng-zong, realistically, can these mediocre projects afford the type of interest rate you charge for two to three years? That is, a compound rate of 20% to 25% a year?"

"No, of course not. These rates are just the indicative, or expected returns, we show to the bank and, more importantly, the fools on the street who subscribe to our fund products to convince them that we can *potentially* get that sort of returns, if and when everything goes smoothly." Deng was proud of his logic.

I queried further, "What if the project cannot go public in three years, and the controlling shareholder, the city government, has to buy back your investment?"

Deng smiled broadly, "Our buy-back side-clause stipulates that they pay us an annual interest of 13% to 14%, instead of our expected IRR [Internal Rate of Return] of 20% to 25%."

"At 13% to 14% buy-back return per annum, how are you going to split the pie with your bank and retail investors?" I challenged Deng.

Deng took out his pocket calculator, "The retail subscriber of the funds gets 5% to 6% depending on our marketing. That is a tad higher than the standard fixed-term deposit rate. But the suckers get the option value when the projects go public in the stock market. The bank gets 3% to 4%, you and I get 1% to 2%, and there will be plenty left to spoil promoters and other middlemen such as lawyers — 1% to 2% for us! When we do RMB5 to 10 billion deals, we will get a tidy fee income of RMB50 million to 100 million each year!" Deng's eyes shone with excitement.

Those were some very tidy calculations. I just wondered if those civil projects could afford to pay even 13% to 14% a year for three years? These were by no means small charges. I reckon some of them would be lucky to find money to repay the principal at the end of the three years. What if there was a default?

"Never mind, Joe. We will get the city government to guarantee the safe return of our money. After all, the common practice these days is to get a piece of commercial land as collateral. If the shit hits the fan, we will repossess the land and build a housing project, or flip the raw land," Deng assured me.

"Why do the banks not set up internal private equity firms to do what the Lucky 15 do? Why do they need you?" I asked.

"Look, banking regulation does not allow banks to engage in direct investment business. That's why they need us."

I was still not convinced I should get onboard with Deng. He was a bit desperate.

He continued on. "Look, I will leave it to you. This is a once in a lifetime opportunity. Your friend Wu Jinhua's PE firm, The

Golden Dew Capital, is also one of the Lucky 15. Check it out. He has made a killing for himself!"

I had already heard that from others. But still I had decided to be less rich.

Who Says Banks Do Not Compete?

While Chinese banks are majority-owned by the government, they do compete fiercely. A banker's life is not exactly a 9 to 5 comfortable job plus fat packages.

What I witnessed in October 2012 can give you a sense of the competition. I was in a Starbucks Coffee in Tianhe District, Guangzhou, waiting for a meeting with a regulatory official. The meeting was delayed and I had some time to spare. So I walked to China Merchants Bank next door to get a platinum credit card which would allow me to get a complementary upgrade to my seats on domestic flights. I already had an ordinary card there, so I just needed an upgrade. I placed my order in a few minutes and was told to come back to collect my platinum Superflower VIP card the next day.

The next day, when I was in Tianhe District for something else, my taxi driver took me to the wrong branch. I could not remember the name of the street or the name of the branch I ordered my card at. Two enthusiastic girls who looked like fresh graduates from college stopped me from going to the right branch.

"Do not bother to find that branch, sir, we will order another card for you and have it delivered to your office tomorrow. It is the same bank, anyway. These are some of our high return wealth management products, and you only need to sign here."

"But it will be a waste to leave that card lying in that branch," I protested.

"Don't worry sir. That card will be recycled in two weeks if you do not collect it." With that, I ordered a new card, and signed up to buy one million Renminbi' worth of Huiji Town Renewal Project Fund.

Like millions of mom-and-pops, I buy these wealth management products via bank branches, and count on the banks to honor the return on my money, as well as the return *of* my money. If the underlying projects go sour as they do sometimes, the banks that marketed those projects will have to absorb the losses. This is a bit similar to the safety of our bank deposits.

Strictly speaking, there is no bank insurance system in China, unlike in the United States or elsewhere. However, the public thinks that the banks have an implicit contract with the government. Depositors have little concern putting money into the smallest deposit-taking entity like a village bank, or a credit union.

This is a dangerous illusion. Only when there is a bank run, or severe stress in the banking system, will the implicit deposit insurance be made more explicit. For now, we just party on.

A day after I got my platinum credit card from China Merchants Bank, I spoke at a conference hosted by Goldman Sachs about the opportunities and risks in the Chinese banking industry. Richard Jackson, head of Ping An Bank, shared his insights as the other panelist with the audience. Jackson was sanguine, probably because his position did not allow him to sound too negative. On the sideline of the conference, I ate dinner with Lan Qi, China Merchants Bank's Board Secretary and one of my alumni from the Graduate School of the People's Bank of China in the 1980s, I told him the story of my platinum card and he was a bit embarrassed about competition between his bank's own branches.

Banks Eat What They Sell

Constrained by loan-to-deposit ratios and annual loan caps, Chinese banks have become eager to boost so-called "fee incomes." One obvious solution is selling wealth management products in their branches. In theory, the banks are simply marketing agents, and are not responsible for either the returns on the money or the return *of* the money.

> // Constrained by loan-to-deposit ratios and annual loan caps, Chinese banks have become eager to boost so-called fee incomes. //

However, in reality, the public pretends not to understand the distinction.

The promotional pamphlets of these mutual funds, private equity funds, and bond funds clearly state that the funds are risky, and that the banks do not guarantee their safety.

No matter. As a protracted legal battle in Hong Kong over Lehman Bonds showed, the public just does not care. After the Lehman Brothers collapse, many investors in Hong Kong lost all their money and embarked on a campaign to have the selling agents (banks such as Bank of China, HSBC, DBS, and so on) make good on the money. Whatever disclaimers the retail subscribers may have seen when they signed up, the government of Hong Kong forced the banks to cough up the dough.

In China, the story is the same. The banks have always quietly absorbed the losses of underlying investment projects whether customers had signed disclaimers or not.

A vast majority of retail buyers of those products know very well that they are making a risky investment bet. However, when things turn sour, the customers will always cry foul. They will stage protests and sit-ins until they get their money back. As a result, the banks have become more selective on the products they market. After all, in any given bank branch, you cannot possibly sell 300 mutual funds or 200 private equity funds all at the same time.

In the past three decades, more than a few small banks, broker-dealers, credit unions, and trust companies have gone broke. But there was never a bank run because without exception these institutions were taken over by other banks. For example, Hainan Development Bank was absorbed into ICBC.

In 2004, Beijing Securities lost all its equity, and still owed customers money equivalent to USD200 million. UBS took over all its licenses and operations, having paid all its customers off. Goldman Sachs did a similar thing when it took over a securities company in Hainan province.

Around the year 2000, the big four Chinese banks also became insolvent, and the central government had to recapitalize them after spinning off trillions of yuan of bad assets into the four asset management corporations ("bad banks") that I alluded to earlier in the book. Subsequent to the recapitalization, these banks made more bad loans, but the massive inflation in China had pushed up their asset value, saving these banks from yet another wave of disaster and recapitalization. Even the four asset management corporations, such as Oriental and Cinda, became viable again.

Junk Bond Agents

In the past three decades, trust companies have had a more humble history. The first trust company, CITIC, was created in 1979 by Rong Yiren, to essentially bypass the banking rules which the government had enacted.

Bank lending in those years was subject to very strict ceilings on interest rates, but the ceilings were not applicable to the CITIC which borrowed heavily from banks to bet on real estate, infrastructure projects, and businesses. If the loans turned sour, it was the government's loss, and when it made money, executives claimed the credit and got the rewards.

When I was at the People's Bank of China in the 1980s, I attended several meetings regarding CITIC-sponsored projects. To me, CITIC was a speculative entity with the Ministry of Finance and the central bank's printing press behind it. Since then, things have evolved, of course, and CITIC has expanded and grown into banking, investment banking, and other sectors.

In the 1990s, several hundred trust companies sprang up across China, speculating on all sorts of assets and businesses, including treasury futures and stocks. Then a wave of them went bankrupt because of the anti-inflationary drive and credit tightening introduced by then-Premier Zhu Rongji.

After the purge, the regulators kept about 65 of them. Today, the name of a trust company is still a misnomer. They do not provide trust products as they are known in the West. They are essentially finance companies or merchant banks. They lend to corporate entities at high interest rates, and more importantly, they raise the funds for a business that would otherwise be unable to borrow from banks at prime lending rates or any rates.

It would be accurate to label trust companies in China as high yield bond houses, or junk bond agents, similar to Michael Milken's Drexel Burnham Lambert in the United States in the 1980s and 1990s.

Of course, there is nothing wrong with this type of business, as there is a genuine need for it.

> **// It would be accurate to label trust companies in China as high yield bond houses, or junk bond agents, similar to Michael Milken's Drexel Burnham Lambert in the United States in the 1980s and 1990s. //**

Under most circumstances, Chinese banks demand both hard collateral and predictable cash flows for their loans, and as a result many businesses do not meet those standards. Trust companies fill the gap, and provide them with a much-needed source of funding.

Most users of trust companies in recent years are real estate developers, mining companies, and industrial companies that have insufficient hard collateral but whose cash flows are reasonably strong. Local governments are also frequent users of trust companies' services as their public works projects generally do not meet banks' lending criteria. The jury is still out as whether these city governments can eventually repay high cost loans. So far, they have relied too heavily on the revenue from selling land. But as is widely known, there is a lot of vacancy and overbuilding in the real estate market so a crisis is always lurking in the background.

8

Chapter

A Perfect Storm of Subprime Credit

What is prime credit or very safe credit? I like to make things as simple as possible. I think it is safe to say that a vast majority of good-quality (or safe) credit customers are in the folds of banks. In addition, banks engage in a great deal of subprime credit.

In other words, everything shadow banking is associated with (i.e., everything outside the regular banking system) is subprime, or can be regarded as subprime.

Alongside microcredit and pawnshops, there is another animal: financial guarantee companies. This creature came into being in the late 1980s, as the Chinese government took a page from the playbook of the governments in the West. In the West, governments have set up various incentive schemes to support small businesses. China's answer was to create financial guarantee companies for small businesses to be able to borrow money at reasonable rates, or just simply to be able to borrow.

Since this objective was partly social and political, it is no surprise that these entities were all owned by the government, or entities associated with the government in the 1980s and even in the 1990s.

Toxic Dumping Ground?

A rising tide lifts all boats. In the growing Chinese economy of the past three decades, most guarantee companies have made decent money, as credit default ratios stayed very low. In recent years, however, some of these entities have been privatized for various reasons. Either the local governments were short of funds to grow these entities, or these entities were run to the ground on the back of mismanagement.

In the 1990s, the private sector became very interested in this sector. Many more licenses were issued to create guarantee companies. At the sector's peak in 2011, there were 15,000 financial guarantee companies across the country. Some estimates even put the number of players as high as 20,000.

The business model of a guarantee company is simple. If a small (and sometimes a big) borrower is unable to meet the banks' lending criteria, due to a lack of qualified collateral or its high gearing ratio, it can approach a financial guarantee company for help. The guarantor will underwrite the safety of the bank's money for a fee, and the bank will approve a loan. Essentially, the bank's counterparty has shifted to the guarantor. If the loan goes bad, the bank can pursue both the borrower and the guarantor.

Of course, the banks do not just accept the promise of any guarantee company. Each bank has its own selection criteria and an internally-approved panel of guarantors. Over time, the modus operandi of the sector has evolved. In some cases, the only thing the managers of guarantee companies have to do is just sit in the office and wait for the banks to call. Naturally, the guarantor has to make its own risk-reward analysis and price the risk accordingly, but if you turn down the business too often, you may receive fewer calls from the banks in the future. So the managers of a guarantee company have to engage in a delicate balancing act. Some more shrewd operators have successfully minimized their reliance on banks' referrals by reaching out to customers directly.

Their skills are tested every day: it is no use to approach prime customers as banks serve them well, and these businesses do not need an extra layer of expense. So, the trick is to find the best possible subprime credit.

Some industry veterans jokingly call financial guarantee companies the banks' toxic dumping ground.

In recent years, changes that have taken place in the sector include the provision of guarantees for corporate bond sales, and the sector's involvement in large loan deals in syndicates, i.e., several guarantee companies team up to share big risks.

Regulation by Seven Ministries

There are both nationally- and regionally-registered guarantee companies. Rules are general and were most recently revised by seven ministries in 2010. These seven ministries were the bank regulator (China Banking Regulatory Commission), the central bank, the Ministry of Industry and Information, the National Development and Reform Commission, the Ministry of Finance, the Ministry of Commerce, and The General Administration of Industry and Commerce. So, everyone has his finger in the pot. However, the day-to-day supervision of the sector rests with the local government's Finance Office, also the regulator of microcredit firms.

Rules for the sector are generous in my view.

For example, guarantee companies can guarantee credit up to 10 times their equity capital at any given time. They must not take deposits, or make loans. Single-customer exposure must stay below 10% of the guarantor's net assets, and exposure to a group of affiliated customers must stay below 15% of the guarantor's net assets. There are also rules about taking provisions for bad credit each year.

There are no rules on fees because there is no such need. Guarantee companies are encouraged to price their risks appropriately. This is where the challenge lies. There are a large number of government-controlled guarantee companies that are generally better established, and better funded than their private-sector rivals. But these government firms tend to be less attentive to risk-adjusted return on investment. This means that they price their risks too cheaply. I am not sure if a certain amount of national service or politicians' pressure is at work here. But I often see credit guarantees priced at 2% to 3% of the total principal of the loan. I have also seen pricing well below 1%. Wansui Micro

Credit has been a beneficiary of this low pricing in the past few years. While some of these guarantees have proven to be safe in the end, they tie up capital and capital is expensive.

As this type of low pricing has existed for a while, it is hard for shrewd private sector guarantors to assert their prices. They often face a tough choice of losing market share or doing deals that they later regret.

I often compare this sector's competitive landscape to that of hotels in China. In all Chinese cities, the government is obsessed with having as many grand hotels in their cities as possible. But the building and running of hotels is generally a lousy business — at least in the current business environment. So when the city government sells land to residential property developers, it often insists that the developers build a grand hotel as part of the land-sale package. Over time, Chinese cities are saddled with too many hotels.

As a result, the room rates can never climb above a certain sensible level. For the property developers, poor returns (or loss-making) at their hotels are tolerable because they get cheaper land from the government, and make extra money from the selling of apartments nearby. But for ordinary hotel owners and operators, this is depressing.

And the pain does not stop.

The financial guarantee sector is in a risky subprime business. They sell credit default swaps. But many managers mistake it for easy money up for grabs. A large number of inexperienced or careless operators have gone bust in the past five years despite a growing economy. High-profile failures include one of the biggest operators in the country (based in Shenzhen) that had attracted significant equity investments from several global private equity firms.

From 2009 to 2011, the sector almost became "the Wild West

of Finance." Opportunities were abundant on the back of a robust economy fuelled by credit expansion, but they were not enough for the inflated greed of many operators. Too many operators exceeded their

> **//** The financial guarantee sector is in a risky subprime business. They sell credit default swaps. But many managers mistake it for easy money up for grabs. **//**

already generous 10 times leverage limit. Many guarantors charged customers fees that were extremely high but not properly booked. Some violated the restrictions on deposit-taking and lending. Many made guarantees for loans, without due diligence on the borrowers, thinking that fees on the guarantee were just freebies.

The chickens finally came home to roost. Large numbers of loans went sour. Many guarantee companies were unable to meet their obligations to make good on the banks' loans. Subsequent investigations exposed a large number of frauds between borrowers, bank managers, and guarantors. Heads rolled and many of those responsible were put behind bars.

As the lead regulator, the China Banking Regulatory Commission tightened regulation of the sector in late 2011 and early 2012. A large number of guarantee companies (estimated at about 5,000 or one-third of all) have been shut down, and many more retreated as they are forced to shrink their exposure to comply with the rules.

Today, the sector is a lot smaller, but it remains a sensible and profitable sector for the careful operators. The rules are still a lot more generous than those for microcredit firms in my view.

9
Chapter

Chronic Inflation and Distorted Banking

The Scary Compounding of Small Numbers

I am a trained economist who's worked in Chinese and foreign banks in various capacities for more than 20 years. But only after I left my research job did I begin to appreciate a small thing: the power of compounding.

Obviously compounding has power but when looked at from a 10-year, or 20-year, or even 30-year perspective, I really and truly begin to appreciate the idea.

As a research analyst, I often looked at year-on-year growth rates. For example, we often talked about consumer price inflation, gross domestic product (GDP) this year over last year, or a listed company's net profit growth in comparison with last year. After doing that type of work for 20 years, you can be forgiven for having a habit of looking only at the last year. Paul Krugman used to ridicule us analysts as "ups-and-downs economists" and I think he had a point.

Recently, I thought about some long-term issues. For example, when I came to work for a foreign bank in Hong Kong in 1994, China's GDP was only slightly more than twice as big as that of Taiwan's. However, in 2012, it had become 17.5 times as big. How did this dramatic change happen in a matter of 18 years?

Two factors: one relatively small and the other huge. The small factor: the appreciation of the Renminbi against the U.S. dollar. The huge factor: the Taiwanese GDP has been growing at an anemic pace (2% to 3% a year), while that of the Chinese nominal GDP grew at a staggering 16.2% per annum.

Yes, 16.2% compound annual growth!

Now, you might say, it is the real GDP that matters but not exactly.

In the long run, China's inflation rates being higher than those of Taiwan should have been reflected in the faster decline of the Renminbi's value against the common currency here (the U.S. dollar). But it did not. That means that the currency was previously extremely undervalued.

The insight I gained from this comparison is that, a small differential in growth rates, if sustained for a long period of time, can make a huge difference. Everyone should know that. But I started to appreciate it only recently.

Alternative Ways to Gauge Inflation

To understand shadow banking and the driving force behind the real estate bubble, I have looked at China's inflation rate, or the change in the cost of living. Given the general mistrust of the official statistics, I have tried to find an alternative solution.

When I was a principal staff member at the People's Bank of China from 1986 to 1989, I earned a base salary of RMB52 per month, and together with subsides, medical care, and paid housing, it added up to RMB130 per month. Today, someone in the same position probably makes at least RMB11,000 in comparable terms (I would say it is more like RMB15,000).

But let's use the smaller number: RMB11,000. That is a growth of 84.6 times in 24 years, or a compound annual growth rate of 20.31%!

Clearly the real economy has not grown at that kind of pace, and the labor productivity of that civil servant has not improved that much. The gap between the nominal wage growth and the underlying labor productivity growth is inflation, assuming that that junior-level civil servant is representative of the whole labor market and I think it is.

This is scary.

If the trend were to continue, it would not be long before every employee was paid millions of Renminbi a year, and a kilogram of cabbage would cost thousands of Renminbi. In other words, the purchasing power of the Renminbi will fall substantially. To the taxpayer, paying for the services of a civil servant like me and whoever is now in my previous position at the central bank is just like a consumption item, similar to a train ticket, or a sandwich.

On that basis, I have chosen to be unscientific and unprofessional. If the Big Mac Index developed by *The Economist* can be used as a good gauge of foreign exchange overvaluation or undervaluation, why can we not use a typical consumption item like a junior civil servant to gauge the change in the cost of living?

The point I am making here is this: economists and observers often argue about whether the government statistics are accurate or not in the short term. But that is missing the point, as it is hard to tell who is right and who is wrong. But in the long term the picture becomes much clearer and one does not need to argue.

From the 24-year nominal wage growth, and the trend growth of labor productivity growth (at a single-digit figure), I suspect that inflation has been running at somewhere between 5% and 10% for the 24-year period. I admit that this is a very wide range, but the point here is that the interest rates on household savings and corporate deposits are significantly below 5%. As most Chinese banks are listed companies, we can see that their cost of deposits is just 2% a year.

Let's take ICBC (the biggest Chinese bank) as an example.

ICBC's average deposit balance in 2012 was about RMB12.5 trillion, with roughly half as corporate deposits and the other half as household savings. The bank paid about an average of 1.82% on corporate deposits, and 2.15% on household savings. On a blended basis, the bank paid an average 1.99% on all its deposits — by far the biggest source of funding. Corresponding rates at other banks are very similar.

This is way below the 24-year (long-term) inflation rate. It is possibly 3 to 4 percentage points below it. You might argue that we must compare the interest rate with the current-year inflation rate. But we do not know what the credible inflation figure is at present, as official statistics have been publicly discredited.

Interest Rates Far below Inflation

If you agree that Chinese savers are paid at a rate far less than inflation, you can appreciate why the real estate market is such a bubble. Despite the government's repeated efforts to clamp down, property prices have stayed high and in most cities continued to skyrocket. Since 2006, the government has introduced many heavy-handed restrictions to stop residents from buying houses and apartments, but people have always found ways to speculate on rising housing prices. The reason? Mortgage interest rates are too low and, as a result, buyers are subsidized to buy and hold onto property. On the other hand, interest rates on deposits are too low, and their purchasing power is diminishing.

These are also the key reasons why credit demand by businesses is so strong, despite poor corporate returns and ever worse cash flows. Borrowers are subsidized to borrow.

Enough has been said about low quality and low value added industries wasting too much energy and resources in China. Everyone seems to know that, and everyone says that they hate the pollution caused by such industries. But why is the government not doing anything real to stop that?

The answer? China is

> **Enough has been said about low quality and low value added industries wasting too much energy and resources in China. Everyone seems to know that...**

addicted to low quality and low value added industries, so much so that the government is afraid of change. So much is at stake: employment, social order, tax revenue, and outstanding bank debts.

When interest rates on deposits are low, depositors are often on the lookout to deploy their cash in some other ways. They discover that some borrowers (outside the mainstream) are willing to pay them far more than banks do. These borrowers are either totally ignored by banks, or the banks do not meet their full demand for credit. As a result, an underground credit market developed.

There are three time-honored bits of wisdom here:

1. Where there is regulation, there is evasion of regulation.
2. Where there are import duties, there is smuggling.
3. Where there are controls over interest rates, there are underground financing channels.

From 1986 to 1989, when I was at the central bank, China was a more political country than today, and Communist ideology deemed the private sector an unfit one in which to conduct financial activities. Any person-to-person lending was regarded as immoral, disruptive, and illegal. But everyone knew that it was always there. Just like prostitution. It was labeled the black market.

Part of my job in those years was to monitor black market fund flows and changes in their interest rates. The work took me to places that were known for black market activities, like Wenzhou and Santou. On more than a few occasions, the central bank saw rising activities as dangerous to the banking system, and arrested lots of black marketers.

Most members of the public either did not understand what was really happening on the black market or did not care. Therefore, they just read or heard whatever they were fed by the government via the media. That's why the microcredit industry today still has a bad name.

At its annual economic forum in Beijing hosted by Sohu.com in November 2012, in response to a journalist's question about widespread bad behavior in that industry, I said, "Sure. There are tax dodgers and other crimes, such as the violation of regulations, in the microcredit industry, but the extent of the crime is no more and no less severe than in other industries. The discrimination against the microcredit industry is absolutely unjustified!"

Since around 2000, despite the absence of legislative changes, the government became more relaxed about small-scale financial activities by private individuals, and even by some corporate entities. As long as there are no complaints by disgruntled residents who have lost money, the authorities usually did not bother to intervene. One regulatory official referred to the black market as a tolerable nuisance, and said that "While you cannot root it out, you can apply some medication to soothe the irritation once in a while."

Despite the de facto relaxation on the regulatory front, however, careful companies have still shied away from direct lending activities. But lending among non-financial businesses is a common thing. When they lend money to another corporate entity, they ask a bank to do so on their behalf. It is called entrusted lending. They take the credit risk, while the bank will subtract a modest fee.

The banks have always been the dominant players in Chinese financial markets. But trust companies, armed with operational flexibility, started to erode the banks' dominance since around 2004. They became the go-to place for three types of borrowers: subprime credit users (meaning they do not meet banks' credit standards), prime borrowers who need additional financing, and those urgently in need of financing.

Trust Companies Invading Banks' Turf

Trust companies operate like securities companies, and pay staff much more generously. Their pay scales are similar to those on Wall Street, despite the fact that they are majority-owned and controlled by the government or government entities. As a result, their business has grown quickly.

According to the China Banking Regulatory Commission, the total outstanding assets arranged and managed by China's trust companies was merely RMB1 trillion as of the end of 2007. This number reached 3 trillion by the end of 2010, and 6 trillion by the end of 2012.

That is equivalent to about 9.5% of the total outstanding credit in the banking society (RMB63 trillion). In other words, loans generated and managed by trust companies have become enormously significant.

Banks' lending capabilities are limited by their capital base, and the lending quotas imposed by the central bank. But the trust companies are only agents and matchmakers. They raise funds for customers from third parties. So, their capital base is not too much of a constraint. For a capital base of, say, RMB100 million, a trust company can potentially raise hundreds of billions of Renminbi for customers. The ratio is 1/1,000 or more. The sector's regulator, also the China Banking Regulatory Commission, started to know the risks, since the trust companies have to ultimately make good on the money they raised from the public if the projects they fund go bad. On several occasions, trust companies did compensate end-investors for the losses they suffered. In 2012, the China Banking Regulatory Commission started to phase in capital adequacy rules.

As a result, many trust companies (for example, Zhongrong 中融) have raised additional equity to support their growing merchant banking activities. As merchant banking was clearly a very profitable business, many corporates (government-owned or otherwise) have fallen over themselves to become shareholders of trust companies.

Banks Defending the Honeypot

The expansion of trust companies continued for some years until banks became alarmed. To protect their honeypot, the banks in 2005 started to offer an IPO Stock Purchase Pool of Funds. The IPO Stock Purchase Pool of Funds was essentially for banks' customers to pool money together to subscribe to hot IPOs. In those years, all IPOs were hot, therefore these pools of money chased all IPOs, and made a lot of money for investors. That, in turn, reinforced the perception that IPO funds were brilliant, and that banks' wealth management products in general could do no wrong.

They are no different to gold funds in the world in the past five to six years. As money poured into gold funds, the price of gold soared, and in turn, as the price of gold soared, it validated the view that gold was an attractive investment, sucking more money into gold funds. Everything seemed to work neatly, of course, until it did not.

These funds in theory were agency products, and the banks simply marketed them for fund sponsors, but given the role the banks played, the ultimate risks rested with the banks.

The IPO Pool of Funds and a wide range of other wealth management products flourished after 2005. Fee incomes also became increasingly important. More importantly, this seemed to be the banks' answer to trust companies' invasion into banking.

The types and the sizes of banks' agency business started to grow rapidly from a low base. According to the China Banking

Regulatory Commission, the outstanding balance of these wealth management products was only RMB1.7 trillion at the end of 2009, but it quickly rose to 4.9 trillion by the end of 2011 and then 7.1 trillion by the end of 2012. Relative to the sector's total outstanding balance of loans, the ratio was 11.3%!

That was even bigger than the assets managed by trust companies. But the China Banking Regulatory Commission did not issue regulatory guidelines until August 2011.

Is this trend dangerous to the banking industry? What are the risks?

10
Chapter

Storms in Tea Cups, or the Beginning of the Next Crisis?

In the previous chapter I explained that the loans which originated and were managed by 65 very thinly-capitalized trust companies amounted to RMB6 trillion by the end of 2012. That figure is equivalent to 9.5% of the total outstanding loans in the entire banking industry. In addition, banks have originated off-balance sheet loans, equivalent to 11.3% of the total loans in the banking industry.

Some analysts have come up with slightly different estimates on the size of these loans. Whatever the figures, the point is that a large proportion of loans are made outside the traditional commercial banking model, and the number of such loans is becoming more significant and alarming each year.

Observers inside and outside China are alarmed by the size of the "wealth management products," and their fast growth. Even Xiao Gang, the Chairman of the Bank of China until March 2013 before being made Chairman of the China Securities Regulatory Commission, the securities watchdog, wrote an article in an official media outlet describing the wealth management products as "Ponzi Schemes." Merrill Lynch analysts also cautioned that a bank-run "could not be ruled out entirely" if shadow banking was not curtailed.

However, I agree with analysts at Macquarie and Standard & Poor's in thinking that, while there are significant risks in the rapid growth of various non-traditional credit forms, the Chinese banking system remains very solid.

Of all the literature I have come across on the risks of the Chinese banking industry, I find Standard & Poor's March 27, 2013 report to be the most balanced and thorough.

Shadow Banking in Perspective

What is shadow banking? S&P has adopted the definition of the

Financial Stability Board (FSB), a coordinating unit within the Bank for International Settlements. In that definition, shadow banking means "credit intermediation involving entities and activities outside the regular banking system."

If that sounds unclear, I have a simpler definition: any financial product other than traditional or straightforward deposits and loans by regular banks.

S&P stresses that its measurement of shadow banking only includes current or actual financial products, and does not include contingent credits such as letters of credit, bankers' acceptances, bank guarantees, and committed credit lines. These things will be included in the measurement only after they are drawn down.

Based on the SFB definition, S&P has identified shadow banking in China as including the following products:

1. Wealth management products which originate from banks, either on the banks' own balance sheets or off-balance sheets.

2. Various wealth management products originating from trust companies

3. Various investment programs originating from securities firms.

4. Entrusted loans (intercompany loans) where non-financial companies use banks as agents to lend to other parties.

5. Corporate bonds, which are unusually small in scale in China compared to developed countries. The complex derivatives products seen in the West are absent in China.

6. Curb market loans which include loans handled by microcredit firms, pawnshops, leasing companies, and intercompany loans that do not go via banks' channels, and loans amongst private individuals.

S&P calculates that the size of China's shadow banking industry was RMB22.9 trillion at the end of 2012, a number that is equivalent to 34% of the total outstanding loans in the banking sector, and 44% of the country's GDP in 2012. Compared to G20 countries and the Eurozone, the size of China's shadow banking is actually rather small. The SFB calculates that shadow banking in G20 and Eurozone nations as of the end of 2011 was 111% of their GDP in that year.

S&P further states that while there is a variety of risk profiles for various shadow banking products, China's shadow banking does not yet threaten to destabilize the country's banking industry, for several reasons.

First, its size is small relative to what is seen in other countries, despite rapid growth in recent years.

> **// The size of China's shadow banking industry was RMB22.9 trillion at the end of 2012, a number that is equivalent to 34% of the total outstanding loans in the banking sector, and 44% of the country's GDP in 2012. //**

Second, banks are still able to refuse to compensate investors for the losses suffered in wealth management products which originated from trust companies, securities firms, and others, even if they were distributed by banks, as ICBC did in June 2012 to an RMB3 billion trust product that it distributed.

S&P points out that corporate China is already highly-leveraged, and that shadow banking only adds to the high leverage.

This is where the risk lies.

S&P states that the two major users of shadow banking in China are in areas with the most risk: real estate development and local governments' infrastructure projects.

Finally, S&P believes that "more than half of shadow banking credits in China could have better risk levels than bank loans."

Shadow Banking Is Not the Real Issue

I agree with analysts at S&P and Macquarie Securities that shadow banking is more a symptom than the disease itself. What is the disease then? I think it is financial repression and the huge hidden costs associated with it.

The major challenge for the economy and the banking industry in the next decade is how to abandon financial repression without causing havoc.

Not to be bogged down by the short-term ups and downs in statistics, let's look at some long-term numbers to see the big picture.

Since I started to work at the central bank in 1986, China's nominal GDP has grown from RMB1,027.5 billion in 1986 to RMB51,932.2 billion in 2012, a surge of 49.54 times. Of course, China did not get richer that fast, and much of the growth has been a monetary illusion.

In the same 26 years, according to the National Statistics Bureau (NSB), China's bank credit has grown 76.36 times and, as a result, the broad supply of money (including cash in circulation, and bank deposits) has jumped 143.94 times! This implies compound annual growth rates (CAGR) of double-digit figures!

For the mind-boggling figures, see the table below.

Growth of loans and money supply in 26 years

	1986 (RMB 1 billion)	2012 (RMB 1 billion)	Cumulative rise	Compound annual growth
GDP (nominal not real)	1027.52	51932.21	49.54 times	16.3%
Bank loan (balance)	814.27	62990.96	76.36 times	18.2%
Money supply (M2)	672.09	97414.88	143.94 times	21.1%

Source: National Statistics Bureau, China

If you think the choice of the beginning year (1986) played a role in the calculations in the first table, we can change the beginning year to 2000. But the results will be remarkably similar, particularly in the compound annual growth rates of bank loans and money supply. The cumulative growth rates are also striking: In a matter of 12 short years, bank loans in the economy have grown 534%, and money supply has grown 604%! See the table below.

Growth of loans and money supply in 12 years

	2000 (RMB1 billion)	2012 (RMB1 billion)	Cumulative rise	Compound annual growth
GDP (nominal not real)	9921.46	51932.21	4.23 times	14.8%
Bank loan (balance)	9937.11	62990.96	5.34 times	16.6%
Money supply (M2)	13835.65	97414.88	6.04 times	17.7%

Source: National Statistics Bureau, China

It is not a stretch to conclude that much of China's economic expansion in the past 26 years (or 12 years for that matter) has been fuelled by credit growth, and that corporate indebtedness has grown much faster than the economy.

Escalation of Credit and Inflation

What is wrong with credit growth running much faster than the real economy? In the short term, it is probably alright, but in the long run, it means several things.

First, it means that the corporate sector's returns of capital are declining.

Second, financial risks are growing due to rising leverage ratios. Too many companies have become too dependent on cheap credit.

Finally, and most importantly, such rapid growth in bank loans in such an extended period of time cannot be explained simply by real economic demand, and there must be other significant factors.

One of the factors I have identified here is parallel escalation of inflation and credit growth: the purchasing power of money is falling which means that you therefore need more money (and credit) to facilitate the same amount

❙❙ The vast majority of wealth management products which the banks offer are merely deposits in disguise.❙❙

of business. On the other hand, as more money (and credit) is created in the system, prices will go still higher, further eroding the purchasing power of money. It has become a vicious cycle.

But how did we get into this mess? Can a free market right itself?

As S&P points out, the vast majority of wealth management products which the banks offer are merely deposits in disguise. As of the end of 2012, these products amounted to RMB7.1 trillion (some 18% bigger than the estimate by Macquarie Securities), equivalent to 7.6% of the banks' total deposits. The average yields on these products were 4.11% in 2012, versus the rates on one-year fixed-term deposits of 3%, and the average cost of bank deposits of about 2%.

Nobody Trusts Banks

Why do the banks willingly offer wealth management products at rates much above their standard deposit rates which push up their average cost of funding? The answer is competition. If Bank A does not play the game, other banks will, taking deposits away from Bank A. To neutralize competition, Bank A also provides the same products.

What will happen if the government were to remove the controls on the interest rates the banks can pay to depositors? The government thinks that would be unimaginable! "How can we ever possibly allow the banks to compete for deposits on prices? The banks would engage in reckless competition, and push the deposit rates skyward."

But why do the banks in other countries not push deposit rates skyward? The answer we often hear from government officials and observers is, "The banks in other countries are not owned by the government, and, therefore, they are more rational competitors."

In other words, the Chinese government does not trust its own commercial entities to behave sensibly.

That is a very strange concept. But if there is one consensus in the whole of China, this is it: Chinese banks are not to be trusted with the power to set their interest rates on deposits.

As alluded to earlier in the book, the grand plan to liberalize interest rates has been announced and reiterated by the government in numerous speeches and documents since 1986.

Today, it is still just that: a grand plan — a rolling five-year plan. By 2013, all interest rates had effectively been liberalized except the rates on household deposits.

If the government and the public do not trust the "invisible hand of the market," there must be a genius or a group of geniuses at the central bank who can regularly set, and adjust, the deposit rates. These rates must be above inflation, and also must reflect the demand for, and supply of, funds.

Sadly, the deposit rates have been too low for too long, and this fact has contributed to the parallel escalation of inflation and credit growth in the past two to three decades. There are enough officials and observers who understand that deposit rates are too low and are probably far below inflation, but there is no political will to change the status quo. The common argument we hear is that corporate China cannot afford higher lending rates, and thus the central bank must keep deposit rates low. The need to create jobs is often cited as another reason. Nobody can argue with it.

Damaging Effects of Low Interest Rates

The government not only controls deposit rates, but also keeps them at artificially low levels. There are three obvious side effects of this policy:

It encourages demand for credit, as the hidden subsidies are hard to resist. This accentuates the parallel escalation of credit and inflation.

It causes undesirable transfer payments: Low interest rates rip off ordinary savers to subsidize those who have access to bank loans. It is a brutal fact that credit rationing is often based on things other than merit.

It creates two credit markets: one for the privileged and the other for the underprivileged. In fact, the existence of the first is the cause of the second one. Limited credit is often fully taken up by privileged borrowers, so relatively weaker borrowers (on the financial or social ladders) have to go to more expensive shadow banks. If the government really wants to reduce the cost of funding for SMEs and underprivileged consumers, it should raise interest rates for those "prime" borrowers. So their demand in that market will decline, creating space for SMEs and underprivileged consumers.

Paradoxically, higher interest rates and lower demand in the privileged credit market will lead to lower interest rates in the underdog market and the improved availability of credit. In other words, the only way for the government to provide financial relief for the underprivileged is to raise benchmark interest rates.

In the past decade, we often heard complaints about unfair competition between state-owned enterprises and the private sector, between privileged private firms and the underdogs. These are understandable complaints. How can you have fair competition when the cost of funding is so vastly different?

The Beginning of the Next Crisis?

Winston Churchill once said, "It is difficult to make predictions, especially about the future." I heed his advice and will not make a prediction here. But I am deeply worried about the negative real interest rates, and the parallel escalation of inflation and the credit explosion in the past three decades. Forget about the 17.7% compound annual growth of money supply recorded in the past 12 years, just look at the much-reduced growth rate of 15.7% reported in March 2013. If this growth rate is sustained for the next 10 years, China's money supply (M2) will rise another 330% from the end of 2012. You have to say it is scary.

With this type of high growth rate year after year, I see social and economic consequences.

Socially, as ordinary savers continue to subsidize privileged borrowers, inequality will become unbearable, if it is not already unbearable. In 1983, when I graduated from the Hubei University of Finance and Economics in Wuhan, job opportunities were everywhere. Though I was an ordinary farmer's son, I was spoiled for choice. The society was reasonably egalitarian. Like all my contemporaries, I was very hopeful of the future. But these days, I cannot say anything exciting to fresh graduates from universities. In my first month at Wansui Microcredit in June 2011, I spoke with some 15 new recruits, and despite my best efforts to sound optimistic about the future and their career prospects, I must have sounded dull and slightly less than frank. I must say, I struggled quite a bit in the preparation of my speech. In the past few years, I have been invited to speak at universities about young graduates' careers and entrepreneurial ventures, but I turned them all down. The only topics I have agreed to speak about are microcredit and the stock market because for the ordinary young men and woman without a lot of assets (political or financial) in China today, the career prospects are not exciting. Competition is fierce, inflation is rising fast, and salaries cannot beat inflation. It's an uphill battle for these young people.

In inflationary periods, asset prices continue to grow fast. But you have to have assets to benefit from this upward spiral. More importantly, you have to have access to cheap finance to maximize your returns. This is where the problem lies. We are often taught about the merits of savings. But in the past few decades, savers have lost out hugely. If you are an ordinary civil servant, a factory worker, or a shop manager, your accumulated savings from your wages will be insufficient to buy you an apartment (or even a down-payment), and many feel they might as well spend all their wages, from paycheck to paycheck. The biggest beneficiaries are speculators who have good access to cheap finance.

Apart from huge income gaps, there is a widening wealth gap. All this is fuelling social discontent. But depressed interest rates, and its twin consequences (credit explosion and inflation) are failing the vast majority of the citizens.

Economically, the depression of interest rates is also causing many problems. There is the housing bubble, industrial overcapacity, and unfair competition between privileged borrowers and other borrowers. Finally, there is the environmental damage.

How is all this going to end? I can only speculate. There are two possibilities: one is a nice scenario and the other a nasty scenario.

In the nice scenario, the central bank recognizes the danger we are in, and raises both the deposit rate and the prime lending rate steadily in a matter of three to five years. This way, the money supply growth will gradually fall to 7% to 8%. As a result, the economy will deflate, and even slide into recession. But as the government toughens it out, a large number of cyclical companies will go out of business, and commodity prices will fall back to the level seen in or around the year 2000. Unfortunately, rising unemployment rates will be a by-product.

In the nasty scenario, the central bank will continue the current course of action. It will only talk about prudent monetary policy, but will not practice it. A crisis will erupt in three possible ways.

One is spreading social unrest.

The second is a bursting housing bubble.

The third is a global economic slowdown that coincides with a domestic recession.

11
Chapter

Investing in the Shadow of Real Banks

Since 2012, shadow banking has been a hot topic. However, the main questions have been: "Is this risky for China's banking industry? And if so, how risky?"

In the previous chapter, I cited S&P analysis that most of the shadow banking products probably have better risk characteristics than regular bank loans. After all, the current size of shadow banking in China is modest compared to that in G20 countries and the Eurozone.

However, there are two much broader issues. First of all, everyone agrees that shadow banking will grow rapidly in the next few years, regardless of any restrictions imposed by the Chinese government.

The question is: what is the key driver for this growth? As I discussed earlier, the key driver is the regulated interest rate that is too low.

Low interest rates and inflation reinforce each other. I believe that the central bank does not want to deregulate deposit rates in the next few years for fear of the banks' irrational competition for deposits on the basis of interest rates. If

> **// I believe that the central bank does not want to deregulate deposit rates in the next few years for fear of the banks' irrational competition for deposits on the basis of interest rates.//**

I am right about that, it is a foregone conclusion that the parallel escalation of inflation and credit growth will continue for some years to come. This credit growth will come from both regular banking and shadow banking.

Additionally, what does shadow banking mean to asset values, particularly real estate and the equity market?

If You Cannot Beat Them, Join Them

Banks are simply the best long-term investments in my view. Those who are negative on the sector generally have two reasons. First, the banks are opaque and you can never trust their numbers, particularly on non-performing loans. Having worked as a bank regulator in the 1980s, and operated a microcredit firm more recently, I can understand that verdict. However, try to name one industry which is not opaque. We must not have exaggerated confidence in any company, be it a cookie maker, department store, or a gas company. They can be equally opaque, if not more so.

Investing in banks is a bit like buying an index fund. Banks are a consolidated statement of the economy. Buying bank shares is like buying the whole economy. The benefits of doing this are clear: you can avoid making a bet on specific sectors or companies and thus avoid their cyclicality and volatility. Sure, banks can be buried in bad debts when the economy enters a severe downturn, but you'd be naïve to think that other sectors will fare much better.

In the global crises from 2008 to 2009, lots of American and British banks went belly up, or were nationalized and rescued by the sovereign governments. In many cases, shareholders were either wiped out or saw their stakes heavily diluted. That was indeed tragic.

However, you wouldn't have had the luck of being bailed out if you were in a non-financial industry. Unless you were General Motors.

Some bearish investors say that Chinese banks are stifling corporate China as they are taking too much profit from the rest of the economy. When the total net profits of U.S. banks accounted for almost 40% of all the net profits of all the listed companies in 2006 and 2007, the result was a global financial crisis.

In China, the ratio has long exceeded that level and is now just over 50%. So, we are in for a major correction.

As they say, "If something is not sustainable, it will stop."

Maybe, but we do not know when and if that correction will take place. After all, the interest rates the banks charge are below the equilibrium rates. The only reason why corporate China (except the banks) has low profitability is because they borrow too much. When returns on invested capital are low, additional leverage only makes matters worse. That is a point Tim Koller and his colleagues made in their 2010 book, *Value: The Four Cornerstones of Corporate Finance.*

It is true that the Chinese banks are guaranteed huge profits by regulated interest rates, but is the status quo likely to change much in the next 5 or 10 years? I don't think so.

Will the current banking regulations kill the non-financial industries if they stay the same? I don't think so.

Leaving the big banks aside, are small banks likely to double their net profits in 5 to 10 years? Sure, and

> // The only reason why corporate China (except the banks) has low profitability is because they borrow too much. When returns on invested capital are low, additional leverage only makes matters worse. //

when they do, that will be pretty decent growth compared to many other sectors.

The current valuation of the banks is attractive. Banks now generally trade at 6 to 7 times their 2012 net profit per share, around 1.2 times price-to-book on average, and they boast a dividend yield of around 5%. Given their growth outlook for the next 5 to 10 years, investors are paid good dividends to wait out.

Non-Bank Financial Institutions

One reason why I took the plunge into the microcredit sector was my bearish views on the banks. I thought that shadow banking institutions should do much better than inefficient banks. I was wrong. The banks have a solid grip on their market, and have low costs of funding. Believe it or not, their management sophistication is also rising compared to my days at the central bank, even compared to just 10 years ago.

I do not derive pleasure from what I'm about to say: microcredit firms, pawnshops, leasing companies, guarantee companies, finance companies, and securities companies have an inferior business model compared to banks. I have learned this the hard way: prime quality customers first and foremost go to banks. Banks generally do a pretty good job at serving these customers. These customers have very few incentives to abandon the banks to embrace shadow banking. Shadow banks have little fighting chance against regular banks.

However, trust companies are a different animal. They are just licensed arrangers of fundraising. If they are careful, they can be enormously profitable and even make the banks envious. However, their high leverage is a double-edged sword — if they suffer a few large losses due to the need to make good on the money lost by the end-investors of their products, their equity could be wiped out.

Let's face it — non-bank financial institutions primarily work in the field of subprime credit. I am not saying that you cannot make money out of subprime credit, but you cannot make more money than the banks on a risk-adjusted return-on-equity basis. When the whole economy has reached such a high cyclical plateau, we face a high risk for cyclical corrections. When those corrections arrive, non-bank financial institutions will bear the brunt of credit losses. Banks will suffer badly too, but they will fare better as they have more cushions in the form of regular deposits, and can price

❝ Trust companies are just licensed arrangers of fundraising. If they are careful, they can be enormously profitable and even make the banks envious. ❞

their loans higher on some borrowers to reflect added risks. But non-bank financial institutions already price their credit highly and those prices have little scope to go higher. Going higher will only scare off customers at a time of economic contraction and weaker demand.

I recently analyzed a well-run leasing company and came to understand why its stock price had not performed in the past few years. I felt that it was unlikely to perform in the next few years. It was a sub-price business to start with, regardless of the company's assertion to the contrary. Apart from their own equity capital, they were primarily funded by loans from banks. Even if the banks treat them as prime customers, they have to borrow at prime rates or around prime.

Banks' lending rates are the leasing company's input costs.

That is a critical issue to understand. If a prime borrower (say, a big hospital) has the choice of borrowing from a bank at a prime lending rate of around 6%, why will it even think about a leasing company that will charge around 9%? There are some minor technical issues for the leasing company to deal with. The leasing company cannot use the money from day one to the full maturity and so some days (often some weeks) will be wasted between drawing the loan from the bank and charging interest from its final customer. The leasing company also has to incur operating expenses and pay taxes. And it also has to deal with delinquent loans (understandably a higher proportion than at banks due to its inferior pool of customers). Add all that together and you can see that the leasing company cannot compete with the banks.

The Real Estate Sector: A Hard Call

My experience in shadow banking and three years at a real estate development company (Shenzhen Investment Limited), have left me with only confusion.

I say this again: *I do not know* what lies ahead for the Chinese real estate sector which seems overvalued, overbuilt, and dangerous. Calling a top is a fool's game and I am not about to do it here.

The physical real estate market does not seem to offer investors the necessary margin of safety. Sure, there are plenty of real estate projects that are attractive, based on seemingly normal assumptions about the costs of construction, finance costs, selling prices, rental fees, and taxes. However, these normal assumptions will prove to be far off the mark if there is a major shift in the macroeconomic landscape. At this juncture, anything is possible — note that the real estate market has been on a tear for about 10 years now.

Real estate developers are one of the two major users of shadow banking products. That is because they have made huge amounts of money in the past decade, and gambling on the future has always paid off. They refuse to believe that there will be an imminent turn of their fortunes.

That is a danger sign.

The willingness of these developers to issue bonds at 10% to 13% annual interest rates shows that these developers are either desperate or very confident of their own profitability down the road. In either case, investors should be cautious.

In general, the equities of these companies trade at a discount to their re-appraised net asset value (NAV) in Hong Kong, and at a smaller discount in the domestic stock market.

They are far more volatile and risky than banking shares.

Given the huge differences in interest rates between Hong Kong and China in

> **//** Given the huge differences in interest rates between Hong Kong and China in the next 5 to 10 years, it is natural that the stock valuation gap of these shares will become very significant. **//**

the next 5 to 10 years, it is natural that the stock valuation gap of these shares will become very significant. Companies that are listed in both Hong Kong and China, while the same companies, have different investor bases. That means that we must use a different discount rate to calculate their discounted cash flows. That method will give us different values for the same companies.

In other words, Chinese domestic stocks will underperform their own H-shares for a long time to come.

Deflating a Real Estate Bubble

In the past five to six years, bearish observers have often sounded alarms on the Chinese real estate market, announcing an imminent crisis every now and then. But such a crisis has not materialized. Indeed, real estate prices have stayed remarkably strong despite the government's clampdown.

These bears include Andy Xie, a well-known China economist, who worked for more than 10 years at Morgan Stanley, and Jim Chanos, a hedge fund manager in the United States who successfully shorted the stock of Enron before its demise.

I can understand their bearish views. But are they calling the inflection point too early, maybe years too early? Maybe continued credit growth (on the back of negative real interest rates) is propping up the Chinese property market?

I do not know when a real estate crisis will occur in China, or if one will actually occur. But this much seems clear:

1. The real estate price is too high for the vast majority of Chinese residents (the affordability issue).
2. The real estate price has risen too rapidly.
3. There is too much vacancy (both sold and unsold units).
4. There is too much construction in progress.
5. The government, unlike in some other countries, genuinely wants the prices to come down or stop rising.

But why is the price stubbornly strong? I think the key reason is the negative real interest rate.

Across the country, large quantities of vacant housing are not only bad for the environment (due to wasted cement, stone, steel, water, and other construction materials), but also to the hard-working savers. Many savers think they are saving wisely because they own an extra apartment, but in reality, the extra apartment (often left vacant for several years in a row) has to be torn down to be rebuilt after 10 or 15 years, due to poor quality construction, poorer maintenance, or city rezoning. For example, many parts of Shenzhen have been designated "old-town rehabilitation projects." The irony is that Shenzhen is a city with only about three decades of history, and many of these "old-towns" were built only 20 years ago!

In December 2012, I published a short essay on my blog, which was subsequently reblogged on many websites. In my essay, I suggested that the government issue a "China Land Bond." The Bond's value would be tied to the real estate price, similar to an inflation-adjusted treasury bond. This bond will allow savers to benefit from rising property prices, or avoid being disadvantaged in the face of property price increases. It will also benefit the country as a whole, as the bond will help keep construction at a necessary minimum and reduce housing vacancies.

In the meantime, the central bank can gradually raise interest rates to carefully deflate the housing bubble without causing a severe economic recession.

Regrettably, my views have attracted little support from opinion leaders as many think the idea of a Land Bond is unworkable.

Investing in the Microcredit Sector

Here is my long-standing analytical curiosity: At any given time, millions of consumers and small businesses are short of funding, and at the same time, large numbers of companies and consumers have surplus cash. Banks typically pay savers (household and corporate depositors) 1% to 3% a year. Most wealth management products command a yield of only 4% to 5%, although there are some outlying products yielding 10% or more. But the yield of 4% to 5% is the mainstream. My questions are as follows: Why do savers (both household and corporate) not invest more in microcredit? Or, why are microcredit firms charging interest rates as high as 20% to 24%, and even 30% per annum? Why are curb-market operators charging as much as 40% to 50% per annum? True, these are profit-maximizing entities, but the fact that these high interest rates have lasted for decades with constant demand deserves an explanation.

Clearly, there is no information asymmetry: these high rates are widely known. Why has more money not flown to consumers and small businesses to bring down the rates?

I think I have found some plausible explanations:

First, the Chinese government only legalized microcredit in 2008, and the public's perception of microcredit (justifiable or not) is still negative to neutral. It will take time for this to change. There is also weak consumer financing, as Chinese culture does not exactly encourage borrowing to fund consumption, though this attitude is slowly changing. Unlike in the West where credit cards are easy to obtain, it is very hard to get a credit card in China, where conditions are rigid. Even though I have lived in Guangzhou for well over a year, I am still not qualified for a credit card because I do not have a permanent residence and a social security number. The facts that I am a resident of Hong Kong and have a high income are not sufficient to get me a credit card in China.

Second, a dominant slice of corporate China remains state-owned despite three decades of economic liberalization. The managers of state-owned enterprises are more concerned about the safety of their money and compliance issues than the yields on the money. In other words, they want to avoid suspicions of impropriety, and protect their careers first and foremost.

At Wansui, I had approached several cash-rich state-owned enterprises with a view to invest their money in microcredit or to buy microcredit portfolios. The conversations never went too far.

Finally, there is insufficient infrastructure to support microcredit or consumer finance, as the sector is still young. Credit rating agencies are a necessary part of this infrastructure. At present, the central bank has a reasonably good system for businesses and individuals, but its coverage is incomplete and it is expensive for microcredit firms to use it. For example, the central bank charges RMB60 to RMB80 for each inquiry in some provinces, and it is off-limits to microcredit firms in other provinces. Its major users are still banks. Sadly, there are no other service providers in the private sector.

Another problem with the infrastructure is that it also lacks credible and proven operators. Most microcredit and consumer finance operators have a history of less than three years and are small. That's just not good enough for consumers and other investors. After all, this business demands trust, confidence, and habitual returns.

In the past three decades, many investors and speculators have made high returns in real estate investment, the stock market, or through real businesses. Therefore, they have high expectations on returns. That's one reason why many savers would rather park their money in a low-yielding bank account, waiting for big opportunities, than invest in microcredit or consumer finance. But that's changing also, as returns are declining in all sectors of the economy.

Since 2012, several broker-dealers and asset managers have approached me to either buy Wansui's microcredit portfolios and/or to get Wansui to assist them in the acquisition of similar assets. I think that is a good start.

The economics behind this business typically work as follows:

Microcredit firms hold portfolios with an embedded yield of 20% to 24% per annum. They sell the portfolios to, say, an asset manager at a return of 11% per annum. (In late 2011, Wansui sold portfolios to Oriental and Pingan Lujiazui Exchange at an all-in cost of about 11.6% per annum)

The asset manager funds the purchase with a pool of funds from its institutional customers or high-net-worth clients. The fund pays clients 6% to 7%, retains 2% to 3% for itself, and spends the final 1% to 2% on lawyers and other things.

But this deal will become unworkable if the asset management firm wants the microcredit company to pay for a credit default swap from a guarantee company, as they typically charge 2% to 3%.

Wansui has generally shied away from the extra expenses of guarantors.

12
Chapter

Mystery in the
Chinese Stock Market

When I came to Hong Kong to work as a junior banker at Swiss Banking Corporation (SBC) in 1994, China's domestic stock market had just gotten started two years earlier. There were less than 100 small-cap stocks traded in the so-called A-Market (for domestic residents), and a few in the so-called B-Market (for foreign investors, and priced in U.S. dollars or Hong Kong dollars).

From 1994 to 1995, as part of the small SBC team, I participated in two transactions: a convertible bond deal for China Southern Glass and a B-market IPO deal for Foshan Electrical, a producer of light bulbs. Both deals were tiny and each raised less than USD50 million.

At the time, stocks listed in the domestic stock markets of Shanghai and Shenzhen traded at 60 to 100 times their annual earnings per share (that is, the so-called price-earnings [PE] ratios). Better sounding and better marketed companies even traded at 200 times earnings. Inflated earnings considered, some companies traded at thousands of times earnings.

It did not matter. Everyone found justification in the robust growth prospects, and believed in the "scarcity premium." The usual argument we heard was "Such a big country and so few listed companies!"

Since then, two major events have happened to the domestic stock market: First, the number of listed companies has grown to about 2,400 (as of March 2013). Second, the valuation has collapsed from ridiculously expensive to just expensive.

Today, most stocks trade at around 25 times PE ratio, and the low valuation of banks that trade at 6 to 7 times PE ratio drag down the market average to about 15 times.

The change of stock market index components (i.e., constituents) sometimes makes it hard to make comparisons of valuation over time, but there is no question that the overall valuation has come down significantly in these two decades.

In light of shadow banking, I am now able to look at the shrinking valuation in the domestic stock market from a new angle.

Regulators' Misguided Role in the Market

It is probably a uniquely Chinese issue: the government and even the watchdog (China Securities Regulatory Commission) always talk up the stock market, and prop up stock prices.

In the early 1990s when the stock market had just come into being, that support was intended to increase the public's awareness of the stock market, and help desperate state-owned enterprises raise money. But increasingly, since hundreds of millions of retail investors have gotten hooked on the market and lost tons of money, the market index has become a political and social hot potato.

In 2013, the government finds itself in a difficult position: it must continue to underwrite the performance of the stocks.

In the past two decades, the government used these instruments to prop up the market. Sometimes, these tactics worked, albeit only for a while, but they always ended in failure.

And the sequence was like this:

1. Politicians and regulatory officials, through media interviews, gave upbeat assessments of the market — usually without much analytical substance. These pronouncements were more like marketing pitches or slogans.
2. Government mouthpieces, such as the *People's Daily*, published optimistic articles on the economy and the stock market. Again, this was invariably propaganda stuff.

3. The government cut stock market transaction taxes and stamp duties for stock trading.

4. There was a suspension of new listings (IPOs) and new share issuances by already-listed companies. This type of suspension sometimes lasted several years. The current suspension started in October 2012, and as this book goes to print, the suspension still continues.

5. From 2005 to 2007, the government acted against all logic to force each listed company's controlling shareholder to compensate free-float shareholders in return for the privilege of converting their shares into freely tradable shares (after a lock-up of, say, three years). Until then, the controlling shareholders' stakes were so-called legal-person shares and could not be traded. This was a major surgery, as controlling shareholders gave free-float shareholders 10% to 20% of their total share holdings. In my view, this was a gross violation of the basic market rule of shareholders' equality. The government forced this down the throat of controlling shareholders because most listed companies were state-controlled and there was a political need to pacify retail investors who had lost billions. The misguided theory that the government had adopted at that time was that the retail investors had bought their shares on the understanding that the controlling shareholders would never trade their shares.

6. Finally, a large number of local governments across China, in order to boost the number of listed companies in their regions, to create jobs, to collect more taxes, have colluded with companies to forge company accounts. In addition, they provided sweetheart deals

to the companies to garnish their earnings in order to raise more funds at IPO. That type of fraud has robbed investors of billions of dollars in the past two decades. Exposure of some of the cases has hurt investors' appetites for stocks.

What Is the Reason for the Poor Performance of Chinese Equities?

It seems counterintuitive that the Chinese domestic equities have performed very poorly in the past 20 years, 10 years, or even 5 years. Almost in any meaningful way, as long as you strip out the irrational euphoria in 2007, this has happened *in spite of* the country's double-digit nominal and real GDP growth, and high liquidity growth. The annual compound growth rate of money supply was 17.7% in the past 12 years, and 21.1% in the past 26 years. Maybe the poor performance of the equity market was *due to* the high growth of GDP, money supply, and bank loans?

My conclusion: in the past two decades, apart from the increased supply of stocks, it is inflation that has dragged down valuation.

How does that work?

Whatever the government does and whatever the public investors pretend not to know, stocks are just like any other assets and their market value is a function of the prevailing (nominal) interest rates. The higher the market interest rates, the lower the asset values will be. This is demonstrated most clearly by the bond market.

As Warren Buffett argues, equities are also bonds, except that these are perpetual bonds. Equities are more volatile, more risky, and less dependable.

As inflation goes up, prevailing (nominal) interest rates also go up (as savers demand compensation for the erosion of their purchasing power). The official control over prime lending rates and deposit rates is a spoiler, but that

> **//** The more severely the banks' interest rates deviate from the "fair" and equilibrium interest rates, the more outrageous the shadow banking interest rates will be. **//**

does not change the fact that the "invisible hand of the market" is still at work. Shadow banking is mostly a reflection of the official mispricing in the regular banking market.

The more severely the banks' interest rates deviate from the "fair" and equilibrium interest rates, the more outrageous the shadow banking interest rates will be.

In a December 2001 speech that Carol Loomis converted into an article (collected in a 2012 book, *Tap Dancing to Work*), Warren Buffett illustrated the negative correlation between inflation and stock market valuation, or the importance of (nominal) interest rates as follows:

Dow Jones Industrial Average
End of 1964: 874
End of 1981: 875
Source: *Tap Dancing to Work*, Carol Loomis, 2012

The Dow Jones Industrial Average moved from 874 to 875 in a matter of 17 years.

In other words, it hardly changed!

In the next 17 years, however, it surged from 875 to 9,181, a 10-fold surge!

Is that because of a stronger economy in the second 17-year period? Not at all. In fact, the converse was true.

In the first 17-year period, nominal GNP (gross national product) grew 373%, while in the second 17-year period, it gained 177%. What then was the driving force behind this very different stock market performance? Buffett attributes it to the change of bond yields, i.e., the market interest rates (see below). Buffett argues that interest rates are inversely related to the valuation in the stock market.

Interest rates, long-term government bonds
End of 1964: 4.20%
End of 1981: 13.65%
End of 1998: 5.09%
Source: *Tap Dancing to Work*, Carol Loomis, 2012

In his May 1977 article published in *Fortune*, "How Inflation Swindles the Equity Investor," Buffett argues that the corporate sector's returns on equity do not change in the long-term — the number has been maintained at around 12% in the United States. Thus returns become less valuable when inflation increases. That aspect of equity is the same as bonds. As product prices go up with inflation, so does the cost of production.

What is the outlook for the Chinese equities in the next decade?

I don't know.

But the big picture does not look too good, as the government does not really have the stomach to tighten the supply of credit to fight inflation.

As this book goes to print, the central bank released money supply figures for March 2013. Broad money supply (M2) grew 15.7% over the same figure a year earlier. While this is slower than the 17.7% compound growth rate for the past 12 years, it remains extraordinarily high given the high base. While Chinese officials criticize the United States for its second round of quantitative easing (QE2), China's own QE7 or QE8 has been well and truly progressing.

If there were absolutely no shadow banking activity in China, and the bank rates were the only rates, depositors would have to accept whatever the banks offer, and corporate China would have to accept whatever interest rates the banks charge. We would be able to use the bank rates as the benchmark rates as the discount rates for equity valuation.

But the genie is out of the bottle.

13
Chapter

Moral and Regulatory Issues

Does microfinance hurt the poor? I don't know. But I can shed some light on the debate with my personal experience. I believe that the public's misinformation and misguided regulations have pushed up the interest rates in the subprime market which has hurt the poor.

If the public and the government are serious about social objectives, they should deregulate the industry.

Definitional Issues Are Cosmetic

To me, microcredit and microfinance are the same thing. Microcredit, consumer finance, pawnshops, and SME financing are just different branches of the same tree. When I became Chairman of Wansui, some of my colleagues asked me to use the term "microcredit" to describe ourselves, because "microfinance" carried a negative connotation. Why? In some developing countries, it's thought that microfinance hurts the poor with high interest rates.

I had to oblige their suggestion.

Later on, I was asked to use "SME financing" to define ourselves whenever possible because we primarily serve small businesses, not consumers.

All these definitional differences are cosmetic in my view.

First, the entities share some common characteristics: they make small loans; credit risks are high, and we normally classify customers as subprime — and the cost of administering these loans is high.

Second, in poor countries like China and India, lending to small businesses is the same as lending to their proprietors. At Wansui, while we mainly lend to small businesses because of their good cash flows, we use the proprietors (instead of their shops) as the borrowers in our contracts. Even in the rare case when we lend to a shop, we require a personal guarantee from its major owner. In many cases, the collateral is the major shareholder's house or other private assets.

Evidence on Both Sides of the Argument

Some passionate supporters of microcredit argue that microfinance firms lift many people out of poverty. Detractors claim that the high interest rates doom poor borrowers to permanent poverty. Both sides can provide a large amount of evidence.

In the 1980s and 1990s, my parents benefited tremendously from the credit union in Maliang Town, though admittedly credit unions are very different from microcredit firms. Credit unions' cheap deposits allow them to charge borrowers very affordable interest rates. These rates are only slightly above prime lending rates.

In my first month at Wansui, my 78-year-old parents made long trips by train and bus to come visit me in Huadu, Guangzhou. While they were impressed and reassured by the young staff of Wansui's three small branch offices, my parents remarked that Wansui was more like a pawnshop from their perspective than a credit union because of the vastly different interest rates. Wansui charged borrowers almost 4 times the prime lending rate. At the time, the prime lending rate was 6% and Wansui's lending rate was 22% to 24%. Some microcredit shops across China charge as much as 30% or 40% effective annualized interest rates and the regulators turn a blind eye to this.

Indeed, it is next to impossible to police the market.

The question is, why do microcredit firms charge high rates? My simple answer is, because they can get away with it.

The next question is, who or what has caused this *seemingly permanent* imbalance between the demand for, and supply of, credit?

First of all, I think the government and the public are to blame. They look down upon the microcredit sector as just marginally better than prostitution and drug trafficking. That attitude is the root cause of overbearing regulations on the sector (including pawnshops, microcredit, consumer finance, and SME lending).

Just look at some of the rules and how they backfire:

A microcredit firm must have more than 10 qualifying shareholders. The biggest shareholder must control no more than 20% a stake.

What do these rules mean? The government's logic is to prevent the biggest shareholder from having too much of a say in the running of the business, or running away with the firms' money.

But these rules are counter-productive. In a new business and private business where shareholders have no exit except to sell stakes to other shareholders, it is costly to find more than 10 like-minded shareholders who are willing to work together for a long time where an exit is elusive (unlike the stock market where you can just flip your shares any trading day). To make matters worse, the government has set high hurdles for shareholders. For example, in most provinces (including Guangdong), you have to be a local resident with proof of income and wealth to invest in a microcredit firm. If you are a business entity and want to be a lead shareholder of a microcredit firm, you have to prove that your business has no less than RMB50 million of registered capital, and has made a certain minimum amount of profit in the past three years. So, many shareholders just inflate their assets or profits in order to qualify. As a result, many such firms are controlled by one family, and other shareholders are only ghost shareholders with no investments who have signed off all rights to the controlling shareholder. In other words, they hold shares on behalf of the controlling shareholder. If the government wanted to encourage fraud and cheating, it has succeeded very handsomely.

Think about the safety of the firms' money. Who has more incentives to run away with the firms' money? Is it someone with a 20% stake or someone with a 100% stake? Clearly the former.

On the operational checks and balances, the government regulation is also misguided. In any business, there must be one controlling shareholder who takes an active role, and other shareholders are just passive. If someone does all the hard work, but only has a 20% financial interest in the success, how high is his motivation? On the other hand, if something goes very wrong, he is only hurt 20% so what is there to minimize the problem of moral hazard? Checks and balances among shareholders sound grand, but that sort of ideal evenhandedness is precisely why the United Nations is such a waste of time, no matter what the goals of the organization itself.

Microcredit firms must not borrow more than 50% of their equity capital.

To me, that is just blatant discrimination. Any normal industrial or commercial business can borrow as much as their creditors will tolerate. Why punish the microcredit industry? Why does the government not leave that decision to the banks? If the government thinks that the banks are too dumb to make that decision, why let them make lending decisions several million times bigger? Of course, the restriction of the microcredit firms hurts their profitability and that cost is inevitably passed on to borrowers in the form of high interest rates.

The China Banking Regulatory Commission bans microcredit firms' loan securitization.

This reduces the amount of money flowing into the sector, thus pushing up the sector's interest rates. For microcredit firms, additional funding will enable them to cut interest rates. But sadly that is not happening due to the Commission's ban. In the early months of 2013, I conducted a straw poll on some microcredit firms. The results were discouraging. Banks have even reduced their lending exposure to microcredit firms. In other words, microcredit firms are borrowing far less than the 50% of equity capital.

The banks are reluctant to allow microcredit firms to serve as loan origination agents.

This also hurts the underdogs' profitability. That will also affect the interest rates they charge borrowers.

The local governments have imposed a limit on the number of licensed microcredit firms, and the geographical areas in which they can operate.

All these restrictions affect the operators' costs and profitability. In turn, they affect consumers and SMEs.

During the January 8, 2012 conference in Beijing where I was named a "Microcredit Person of the Year," I gave a short speech. I offended the officials and some operators in the audience by saying that "The number one objective of microcredit firms is to maximize their profits." I really meant it and my provocation was intentional.

At many previous gatherings, officials and many operators had taken the moral high ground and talked only about "serving the poor and the community." But the inconvenient truth is that microcredit firms are neither nonprofit NGOs nor charities. Their mission is no different from banks, or restaurants, or gas stations.

One official asked me after my speech, "What is your break-even point at Wansui?" I replied, "Wansui will break even if we charge a 7% interest rate."

"Okay then so why do you not charge borrowers just 7% or 8%?"

I shot back: "Have you looked at the break-even interest rate for a regular bank, or the break-even price for a restaurant or a retail shop?"

The reality is that if microcredit firms do not make enough money, their shareholders will exit the industry, and their employees will not be paid well enough to stay, and new firms will not enter the industry. Therefore, the supply of microcredit will dwindle, and interest rates on the subprime market will go higher.

The microcredit industry should not have to bear the burden of "lifting the masses out of poverty." That is an impossible mission. Microcredit is just a business, like any other business. Does it hurt the poor? I don't know. But an equally funny question is, does a department store make consumers poorer?

Let's talk about some misconceptions about this industry.

Like myself before I joined the field of microcredit, people often seem to have some preconceived notions about the microcredit industry. The most common was about how much money the business made. People usually underestimate the huge expenses involved in running small-scale businesses.

In my time at Wansui, I often got calls from people or companies who had spare cash to deploy. They wanted to lend money to Wansui, or buy Wansui's loan portfolio at an interest rate of 15%, or even 20% per annum. I was speechless.

We lent to our final customers at an interest rate of 20% to 24%. When demand is slack, we even lend at 15%. If we took in funds at a 20% or even 15% interest rate, and add in the expenses of lending it out, paying taxes (both turnover tax and profit tax), writing off inescapable bad loans (say, 3% to 5% of total lending value), and slack time wasted (we could not lend all the money out in one day and recall all the loans back in one day), we would lose a lot of money!

The other thing that I have witnessed time and again in those two years was politicians and bureaucrats paying lip-service to our business. They often come to Wansui for a visit, and praise our contributions to society and the poor, underprivileged borrowers. They promise to ask the government to reduce our tax burdens.

But, as you can guess, nothing of that sort ever happens.

I have seen that tax concessions did get passed onto microcredit firms a few rare times. What we do not know is how much time has been wasted in going through the bureaucratic process, how many rounds of golf have been played, and how many financial benefits have been extracted from the "beneficiaries" by the officials involved.

I must say I'd rather go hungry than try to do those things.

Is my industry of choice without immorality? Of course not.

Are we above the hard business practices of other industries? No, of course we aren't.

The second day that I was at Wansui, I was greeted at 8 a.m. by two strangers on our doorsteps. This father and son, who were Wansui's customers, ran a nearby Cantonese restaurant. They said that they just wanted to say hello to Wansui's new Chairman. Clearly my colleagues had told them about me. The father was grateful for Wansui's help in the past and asked if his 17-year-old son could work for Wansui for some weeks, just to learn the ropes.

I can tell lots of stories about satisfied customers. However, a business is a business. We have also repossessed some borrowers' collateral and pressed other borrowers really hard to repay our loans plus interest. We have sued six or seven borrowers in the past three years. These numbers make up just a small fraction of our total number of our more than 3,000 customers including repeat borrowers.

Are heavy-handed bullying tactics involved in loan collections? Not at Wansui. In fact, I'd say that well over 90% of microcredit firms comply with regulations and are not involved in those unspeakable activities. However, there certainly are bad guys among both licensed and unlicensed lenders that give the industry a bad name.

Other illegal activities in the industry include charging interest well above the permitted 4 times prime lending rates. The lenders dress up the extra charges in the form of management fees, or deduct interest charges at the time the loan is disbursed. Or they charge monthly interest instead of a lump sum payment at the loan's maturity. Of course, in doing this, the lenders take on extra risks.

Two years ago, I invested in an equity stake in a Hubei-based microcredit firm. After I learned about such tactics over there, I sold my stakes to the majority owner. Getting out was a relief to me.

Despite these instances, the overwhelming truth is that microcredit is a legitimate business that meets a legitimate demand.

It's as simple as that.

There are more fundamental reasons why some people are poor, and microcredit is certainly not the main reason.

14

Chapter

Alibaba Finance,
China's Future

While I was writing this book, two major events occurred. Margaret Thatcher died and Alibaba Finance, part of the giant Chinese e-commerce group controlled by Jack Ma, lodged its application to the securities watchdog (China Securities Regulatory Commission) to securitize its loan portfolio (a kind of collateralized bond issue) via Dongfang Securities.

These two events are unrelated. But both Margaret Thatcher and Alibaba are very important to China and particularly its shadow banking industry.

In 2011, I visited Simon Hu, head of Alibaba Finance. An experienced banker at China Construction Bank, Mr. Hu patiently explained his grand vision for microcredit. Months later, we had a few follow-up discussions. Alibaba had secured two microcredit licenses, one in Zhejiang Province and the other in Chongqing, though strictly speaking, its online operations did not need such licenses.

Alibaba operates an online e-commerce platform which has a huge number of small merchants buying and selling products and services on it. Given the electronic record of these merchants, and the stickiness of these merchants, Alibaba is uniquely positioned to provide these merchants with loans at a competitive rate and at unbelievable speed. At the same time, its loans will remain very safe, much safer than those players that rely on foot soldiers. The ability of Alibaba to lend money to its online merchants is the biggest reason why the other 6,000 microcredit firms combined cannot possibly compete with Alibaba.

Other online e-commerce companies such as Jingdong (360Buy), Suning, Dangdang, and Tencent have studied the online microcredit market. But until now, none has started in this line of business, probably because their competitive position in e-commerce is considerably weaker than that of Alibaba...and partly because of the government's negative stance on the sector.

Alibaba's securitization of its loan book will be equivalent to it having the power to take deposits. I see great potential on this front, particularly if other e-commerce companies start to launch their own microcredit businesses on the back of the encouragement of securitization.

Together these e-commerce companies are already doing China a huge favor by shaking up the business establishment. As Chairman Jack Ma of Alibaba says, if the banks do not shape up, they will be forced to.

In previous chapters of this book, I noted that the China Banking Regulatory Commission is extremely cautious on shadow banking in general and microcredit in particular. However, the securities watchdog, the China Securities Regulatory Commission, for its own reasons, has dipped its toes in the water with guidelines to securitize financial assets including microcredit portfolios. While it is too early to say if this marks a new avenue for the 6,000 microcredit firms, the trend is clear.

Given the protracted weakness of the domestic stock market, and the huge overcapacity in the 115 securities companies and 100-plus fund management companies, it has become imperative that the China Securities Regulatory Commission create a new revenue stream for its constituents to stay afloat. The domestic bond market and the subprime debt market (including microcredit securitization) have come into view. The former chairman of the China Securities Regulatory Commission has spoken enthusiastically about "business innovations."

Now the question is: Are there enough qualified microcredit assets to securitize? Maybe not.

At this stage, most microcredit assets lack standardization as well as volume and these are the two critical requirements for securitization. But even short of securitization, these microcredit assets can be used as collateral for additional loans, effectively pushing microcredit firms beyond the constraints of their own capital and the 50% limit on their leverage ratio, provided that local regulators (the finance departments) do not sabotage the transactions.

I am optimistic that something will happen on this front, given the competition between the two regulatory agencies (China Securities Regulatory Commission and China Banking Regulatory Commission) and the pressing need to create revenue for the hundreds of thousands of starving brokers and asset managers.

In 2012, both Alibaba and CreditEase completed a handful of securitization deals via trust companies thanks to their political clout. But these were probably the only deals in the sector. The 6,000 other micro credit firms did not have the privilege of raising funds via trust companies.

A Country of Licenses

Some commentators have labeled China a country of licenses and joked that, in the future, even walking in the street will require a few licenses. Government departments like to issue licenses and citizens flock to licenses the moment a license starts to be issued, sensing that it has a certain franchise value, albeit if that's unclear to begin with.

A case in point: When the government legalized the microcredit industry in 2008, thousands of applicants rushed to lobby for such licenses, even without management teams or the slightest idea of how to go about running a business. Sure enough, over 6,000 such companies have mushroomed across the country four years later. Up to 100 license holders still do not have the teams to even start businesses a year after obtaining licenses, while a few dozen licenses have been revoked so far.

Doing business in China has become a costly pursuit due to

licenses, approvals, regulations, and arbitrary official decisions. Wansui, the tiny microcredit firm that I used to run, has to deal with three layers of government on the most mundane matters such as opening a branch in its own district, let alone in other districts, and changing its chairman, directors, and shareholders.

In her tenure as the British Prime Minister, Margaret Thatcher achieved many things. In my view, at least three of her major achievements are particularly relevant to China today.

First, she aggressively privatized government enterprises (British steel, gas, water, transportation, and a host of other industries).

Second, she deregulated the financial sector and made London a much more efficient, competitive, and thus important global financial center.

Finally, she substantially reduced the power of the trade unions, and resisted the urge to pay more attention to her poll ratings.

Clearly, China badly needs a Margaret Thatcher, or someone of her caliber and vision. Regrettably, talking about risk control has become too fashionable in China, and it's now an excuse for government departments to throttle businesses.

First, state-owned businesses have grown significantly in the past 10 years thanks to the government's heavy investments funded by tax revenue and bank loans. They not only have ready access to finance, but their cost of finance is much lower than that for the private sector which creates an unfair playing field. The situation is much worse than in the United Kingdom in the 1980s.

Second, well over 95% of the Chinese banking industry is in the hands of government banks. While they do compete with each other, they pay scant attention to the struggling small businesses. This situation is much worse than in the United Kingdom in the 1980s.

Finally, while trade unions are just a function of the Chinese government (unlike the British trade unions). The rising number of Chinese civil servants and state workers and their permanent employment status are hurting the efficiency of the economy and social equality.

Shadow banking came into being to serve small businesses and the consumers who had been ignored by regular banks. But the survival and prosperity of these shadow banks is often under threat.

So far, Alibaba and other e-commerce companies have largely escaped onerous regulations. Let's hope they continue to thrive, and further shake up and restructure China's business establishment.

Epilogue

Money, Status, and Family

In Hong Kong, money and social status are probably the two most important things in certain circles, including the circles I usually find myself in.

In the staid world of banking, I've been seen as a rebel, a non-conformist, and the odd man out.

Initially, I tried to conform but after a while I just gave up on that idea. Hong Kong is a big enough place to accommodate differences and it's been my home for nearly two decades now.

Resigning from investment banking and walking away from UBS allowed me to thrive in a smaller world of financial business, and I've been comfortable here. Rebel or not, I have been aware of status and money for some time thanks to my childhood.

A Second Class Citizen in the Bush

I was born into a farming family in Jingmen, Hubei Province, in central China in 1963. Due to good natural endowments, such as the fertile land and rivers and lakes near my village, my grandparents and parents lived hard lives but they were self-sufficient.

However, despite their simple lives in the countryside, social status has always been a big thing for me and my family.

Dengren, my grandfather, was luckier than most of his contemporaries as he went to school for a few years when he was young. This education put him on the path to becoming a Nationalist Party leader in the Jingmen region, and he briefly served as the government head in the county.

Financially, his family was probably marginally better off than most. That is to say that he could afford to send his only son, my father, to school for a couple of years when my father was 13, just before the end of the civil war in China and before the Communists assumed control of the country in 1949.

In 1949, when the Nationalist Kuomintang Government (KMT) was forced out of China to Taiwan, my grandfather was too sick to follow the then-ruling government troops to Taiwan.

Under the new Communist regime, my grandfather's background was a sort of stigma and a source of agony for himself, my parents, and, later, me and my brother and sisters.

There were nearly three decades of ideological and political cleansing in China after 1949. When I was around 8 or 9 years old, I would sometimes see some unfortunate old villagers handcuffed, paraded through town, humiliated, and tortured. The only reason was that they or their parents had been rich landlords sometime earlier, or they had played a role in the former government of China.

I only saw my grandfather suffer this type of ordeal in public once. I cried and felt very frightened as well as humiliated. I only vaguely knew that he was treated like that because of his "sins" in the Nationalist Government.

There might have been other occasions when he was tortured, but I did not know about those, and I was smart enough to never ask him or my parents about such things. I told myself that I could not choose my parents, let alone my grandparents.

My grandfather was a very kind elder in the village. I loved him dearly. I could never thank him and my parents enough for their deftness in navigating political matters. Despite my grandfather's background in the former government, his family was only classified as "Rich Farmer," the second worst class.

My grandfather sweet-talked the Communist government to give him due recognition for his reformist efforts. For example, he had become a carpenter, helping to build houses and furniture for more than a dozen poor families for free for a few years.

In other words, this should have demonstrated that he was truly just another poor hardworking villager. He served the people of China whether it was the KMT or the Communist Party in charge.

By the time I was 16, he had become frail, but he would still go and help young families build houses.

Back then, the rural class system in China was a bit like the caste system in India, except that in China it was a political system and one which was based on a subjective judgment on one's family's financial status before the Communist revolution.

This meant that the children were always paying for the sins of their parents, or maybe being rewarded for their family's earlier loyalty.

The worst social class to be part of in the countryside was "Landlord," followed by "Rich Farmer" and then "Middle Farmer." Expectedly, for the Communists who were building the New China at that time, the most glorious top class was "Poor Farmer." Poor Farmers seemed to have the right to berate those in the "lower" classes for having had toxic family backgrounds and the bad misfortune to have had some material success prior to 1949.

How I wished that my grandfather had never done what he did in the old government. When other kids in my village were pampered to join the Communist Youth League, my siblings and I were left out, and we envied those other kids. My parents and my elder sister encouraged me to excel at school so that I could eventually join the Communist Party so that the other villagers would no longer bully us.

The Urban-Rural Divide

There was another dimension in the Chinese Caste system: In those three decades, Chinese citizens were classified into two groups: urban and country residents. This was not just a loose or random classification in statistics. It meant a lot — or everything — for many families. And it still does even until this day.

The residence restrictions had been extremely rigid, mainly so that the government could keep an iron grip on power. Country residents were second-class, and were not allowed to live or work in towns or cities. Differences existed in medical care, education options, food supplies, employment opportunities, and so on.

I knew of my inferior status early, as Maliang Town was just five kilometers away from my village and those lucky people never had to work the rice paddies. In Maliang Town, the people would receive stable monetary incomes every month, come rain or come shine.

When I entered secondary school at the age of 13, several fellow students were from Maliang Town. Their background and knowledge were better than mine. They played different games, spoke differently, and knew things about life.

My inferior complex was starting to hurt me. Despite my good academic results, I knew that I and most other kids from the nearby villages would have to go back to plough the fields after graduation, while these few lucky kids would, as a matter of course, get comfortable government jobs minding shops or grain storage facilities. They might even get jobs writing nonsensical propaganda stuff.

As I stood looking at those Maliang Town kids and listened to the way they talked, I could see my possible future and, at that moment at least, life seemed very unfair to me.

I dreamed about changing my social status but I didn't have a chance…unless, of course, I magically got a place at a university.

In 1979, fate smiled, and I was the only graduate from my high school to enter university. In fact, I was the only graduate from that school to ever enter university, and a few years after I graduated, my old high school was downgraded to a middle school. Until I was told of my university admission, I had only dreamed of going to college. Reading my books as a kid, the word "university" had seemed so distant and so elusive.

But now I was embarking on a new path out of the countryside.

University education and subsequent employment at the central bank changed my social status. Now I not only was officially a city resident, but also a Beijing city resident. That was a heck of a deal at that time!

In 1986, I started to work for the central bank's head office in Beijing as part of the "Emperor's Service Team" after a three-year education at the graduate school of the central bank. My family's low social status did not matter any longer.

Call me status conscious if you like, but I had worked hard to persuade senior officials at the central bank to admit me into the Communist Party. I worked hard at my coursework, played ping pong even though I hated the sport, and wrote numerous letters to senior officials to show that I had broken away from my grandfather's old history.

I finally succeeded in 1985. It was a huge triumph for my family. As there was no telephone access in my village, I had to send a telex to my father to tell him about my achievement. He promptly rewarded me with a postal remittance of RMB110. On the message column of the remittance, he wrote: "Buy yourself a bicycle." That amount of money was indeed enough to buy a Forever bicycle. The price of that brand had probably not been adjusted for three decades.

As I bought the bike, I thought how that amount of money was more than my father's annual savings. As he had just turned 50, he could no longer work the fields as productively as he had before, and the work of a carpenter was also becoming too much for him.

I was guilty as well as excited to receive the money and buy that bicycle.

Microcredit in the Countryside

My work as a regulatory official at the central bank often took me out of the city into the far-flung parts of China on investigation trips. I was always fascinated by curb-market loans and rural credit unions. From 1983 to 1989, I became close to the credit union in Maliang Town. My parents and all the villagers were made members (unit-holders) of the union, a cooperative entity, when it formed in 1958. Everyone had been given 10 shares for RMB10. The plan was to take the deposits from the farmers and make loans to them.

The plan, like others from the Communist blueprint, was Utopian in concept but a failure in practice. After the union was formed, it immediately became another plaything of the few local officials and union managers.

Nationwide, the credit union industry had been bankrupted by mismanagement several times over and only the central bank's printing press was able to rescue it.

In late 2011, when I was at Wansui Micro Credit, I served as an advisor to a businessman from Guangdong on the negotiations to acquire a chain of rural credit unions in Anhui Province. Their insolvency and heaps of bad debts reminded me of the misery of many other credit unions across China, including the one in Maliang Town in the 1980s. I have not visited the Maliang Credit Union since then, and do not know the town's fate. But under the current regulatory regime, the sector's demise is only a matter of time.

Why do I make such a pessimistic and bold pronouncement?

The government limits the geographical area in which any credit union can operate. Each village or township has only one credit union, and that credit union can only serve that small area. This rule hasn't been changed since 1949. The result is that thousands and thousands of credit unions in China are monopolies, but tiny and weak monopolies.

These credit union monopolies are not allowed to expand their businesses into other regions, and therefore they stay very small. Consolidation is impossible and banned. They are not allowed to compete with each other and they are all fragile. If one small area is dominated by, say, mushroom farming, the credit union in that small region will be at the mercy of the ups and downs of the mushroom crops that year. In a neighboring town, if palm oil is the dominant produce, then the credit union in that region will be a captive of the palm oil market.

In recent years, some rural credit unions have been corporatized into much bigger rural cooperative banks. That is major progress. In fact, Chongqing Rural Commercial Bank is such a creature, and I love it. I have even made it my biggest personal investment.

But the old rule and method of regulatory thinking on rural credit unions have been extended to microcredit since 2008.

For example, each county in Guangdong is allowed to set up one microcredit firm and that firm is not allowed to expand elsewhere. In the past year, we have seen some very limited relaxation of the rule, but the outcome will be the same.

Thousands and thousands of tiny and fragile players in the microcredit field keep doing business and trying to survive all across China.

What should the government do to really help the microcredit industry as well as the struggling SMEs and sub-prime consumers?

I think several modest steps are necessary.

First, increase the leverage ratio for the sector from 50% of equity capital to 100% equity capital. This is what many local governments have called for. But only the bank regulator is resisting.

I calculate that this change alone will increase the sector's return on equity by about 2%, and increase credit availability by about RMB100 billion.

Second, allow microcredit firms to open branches wherever they like. This move will broaden their customer bases, and thus lower the risk for customer concentration. Competition amongst microcredit firms will also enhance the sector's efficiency, and may actually bring down the interest rates borrowers pay. Some consolidation among players will ensue, but that will be healthy. It will boost the sector's average efficiency. Approximately 6,000 tiny firms in a small industry mean a lot of repeat work.

Third, the bank regulator should give the green light for trust companies to assist microcredit firms in loan securitization. Whether they do it or not should be left up to them.

Finally, the bank regulator should make a definitive and positive statement about banks collaborating with microcredit firms. The precise terms of the collaboration should naturally be left to the grassroots entities to work out.

Insecurity and Anxiety

In my first couple of months at Wansui, I enjoyed the change and the excitement associated with the new challenges. But what was my long-term plan going to be here?

My wife Lillian had quit her job as a private banking client advisor in 2008 to take care of our two small children and she subtly reminded me that we lacked steady monthly incomes. She wondered about our future. I only vaguely said that we would use Wansui as a launching pad to grow our business.

One evening, she came home from a kid's birthday party at the Chinese International School and relayed the snide question of a snobbish mother. The woman had asked how I was doing and wondered if my microcredit field was really a business.

Just a week before, my 9-year-old daughter had also asked me if I had really become a "small loan shark." I started to put the pieces together. I considered my wife's words and thought about what my future would be at Wansui.

I am not naïve. I know that both money and status are critically important everywhere, not just in Hong Kong. I do not want to sound negative about people who have certain views about how much money you make and what your social status is. We all do a bit of that, don't we?

Lillian had opposed my taking the plunge into the microcredit field and my departure from investment banking too.

Five years before I landed at Wansui, she drove me to work on my first day at Shenzhen Investment Limited, a listed company. I had just left UBS and we walked into my office in Tsim Sha Tsui, Kowloon, together on that first day.

Lillian checked out my simple office and put my day-planner and a dictionary on my desk. When I walked her downstairs to the lobby, I saw a tear in her eye.

"What is wrong with working in IFC?" she asked. "Why do you want this?"

I thought about what she said. Had I made a mistake by giving up what others in Hong Kong were fighting so hard to achieve?

In June 2011, when I left UBS the second time (in fact it was the third time as I had worked at Swiss Banking Corporation in 1994 up until it later merged with S.G. Warburg in 1995), she was more pessimistic.

Thinking about things in terms of my family, she might have been right.

In 2011, after the first few months of my honeymoon with the media and curious investors, I found myself in a disinterested, intransigent, and even hostile regulatory environment. In the morning when I opened my window in New Donghao Hotel, I did feel helpless sometimes. Occasionally, I felt that my efforts were meaningless.

Lillian was born in Nanjing City, capital of coastal Jiansu Province. Her parents both worked as engineers at Sinopec. The second of three children born in the 1960s, she had had a tough childhood. Money was always short. Her parents, who both worked full-time, could not take care of three kids. When she was five, she had to be sent from Nanjing to Tianjin to live with her grandfather and the families of uncles and aunts for five years.

In 1989, after graduating from Shanghai University of International Economics, she worked a few years in Shenzhen before migrating to Canada, and later she received an MBA degree from the University of Indiana in 1999. She then came to Hong Kong to work for the wealth management departments of UBS (where I met her), Merrill Lynch, and Morgan Stanley.

Like me, Lillian was often paranoid about money running out, even after we had saved a lot by most people's standards. Working for genuinely wealthy individuals for almost 10 years might also have colored her perspective.

Having lived hard lives as kids, we both know the value of being frugal. I know that most people think that those in our circles make big bucks at work and through investments. To them, saving money is not nearly as important. I sometimes wonder why some younger bankers who I've worked with would spend very large proportions of their incomes to rent big apartments, or travel business class on holidays, or drive fancy cars. I could not bring myself to do those things even when I made more money.

Maybe, the bull market has been with us for too long? My friends refuse to think about the possibility of a protracted recession or harsh living conditions.

Advisory Work Outside a Bank

Having relinquished Wansui's day-to-day managerial responsibilities, I came back to Hong Kong in August 2012 to plan my next act.

Lillian has made it clear that she would prefer that I go back into investment banking. A couple of banks have also inquired if I would head their research departments. One bank asked if I would lead their real estate banking business. A hedge fund startup also invited me to join them.

I appreciate these offers and suggestions. However, I no longer have the passion for sell-side research. I consider that work too restrictive, and too much selling is required. Some people say that sell-side analysts are glorified salesmen. They have a point. I liked selling, and did that work for 11 years, but I do not want to do it again.

Daniel Tabbush, my former colleague at both UBS and CLSA recently wrote his story after leaving the industry he served for two decades. In *Quit & Run: My Wake Up Call on Wall Street*, he said that the three magic words you never hear from sell-side analysts are "I don't know." He's right. I never felt comfortable saying those three words when I was a research analyst. I even admitted as much in my 2011 Chinese book *The Confessions of A Stock Analyst*.

I also find the time given to research analysts too short. For example, they have to predict 12-month target prices. That is too hard in my view. A good company or a good stock often takes much longer to prove itself.

Investment banking is a better paid field, but it also involves too much selling. I am not against selling per se, but when overcapacity is so outrageous in the industry, excessive competition can be depressing.

Sure, I want to make more money, and bankers are still well-paid but I sometimes think that they are overpaid. I have benefited from the industry for years, and am happy to "create" a job for someone else.

I must make one small confession. After I had enthusiastically worked for a corporate client to raise money in its IPO or a bond sale, and later I found them not as good and trustworthy as I had thought they were, I felt bad. If I were still a research analyst, I would probably publish a very negative report, even risking another court case.

My Current Situation

After I got back to Hong Kong, quite a few listed companies offered me nonexecutive directorships. Obviously, many people still like my inquisitiveness and outspokenness. After analyzing my ability to make a modest contribution, I accepted five of them, one of which is Nanjing Central Emporium which is listed on the Shanghai Stock exchange. The other four are listed in Hong Kong. I also became an independent director of a money management company, China Resources Yuanta Fund. In addition, I have accepted directorships at two companies that are on the path to IPOs.

My schedule has become slightly busier after a few slack months. I took on advisory work for some listed companies. I helped a private company sell a cement plant, and helped a listed company whose stock is illiquid raise money in the form of a convertible bond. I also played middleman for two companies to merge: one is listed and the other private.

Interestingly, these are exactly the types of projects an investment banker does. But their size is too small for bankers to bother with.

Appendix

Major Players in China's Shadow Banking

Five regulators

The China Banking Regulatory Commission (中國銀行業監督管理委員會) is a spin-off from the People's Bank of China. It regulates banks, trust companies, finance companies, leasing companies, consumer finance companies, and credit unions.
Official website: http://www.cbrc.gov.cn

The China Securities Regulatory Commission (中國證券監督管理委員會) regulates securities companies, fund houses, futures exchanges, and stock exchanges.
Official website: http://www.csrc.gov.cn/

The People's Bank of China (中國人民銀行) is the central bank charged with the responsibility of monetary policy. But it and the bank regulator, the China Banking Regulatory Commission, jointly legalized the microcredit industry in 2008. The draconian regulatory guidelines they released have been copied mindlessly by various local governments that regulate the microcredit industry.
Official website: http://www.pbc.gov.cn

Commerce Departments (商務部) and Public Security Departments (公安局) of local governments regulate pawnshops.

Finance departments of local governments regulate micro credit companies, and guarantee companies (those that sell credit default swaps).

Notable players in microcredit

China Development Bank (國家開發銀行) is a development bank owned by the central government. It has numerous overseas branches and entities. But inside China, it has a relatively small office in each capital city, and supports developmental projects. In the microcredit industry, it is the most visible lender. Wansui has received its support since inception.
Official website: http://www.cdb.com.cn/

Hanhua Financial Holdings (瀚華金控) has microcredit firms in five cities: Beijing, Tianjin, Chongqing, Chengdu, and Shenyang. It also operates guarantee companies.
Official website: http://www.hanhua.com.cn

Noah Private Wealth Management (諾亞財富) is one of many numerous third-party arrangers of fundraising.
Official website: http://www.noahwm.com

Ping An Group (中國平安集團) is a financial conglomerate encompassing a bank, an insurance canpany, a broker-dealer, a trust company, and so on. In addition, it has a small microcredit company in Shenzhen. But far more importantly, it sells credit guarantees through its insurance arm to banks that in turn make consumer loans or SME loans. Finally, it has a Shanghai Lujiazhui Finance Exchange capitalized at RMB400 million, doing online matching of microcredit borrowers and lenders.
Official website: http://www.pingan.com

Zengdai Credit (證大速貸) is based in Shenzhen and majority-owned by Zengdai Real Estate Company.
Official website: http://www.zdcredit.com

Zhongan Credit (中安信業) is majority-owned by Paul Theil, an investment manager at Morgan Stanley and a former United States diplomat.
Official website: http://www.zac.cn/

Zhongxing Micro Finance (中興微貸) is seeded by ZTE, based in Shenzhen, and headed by Tang Xia who used to work at Zhongan Credit, China Construction Bank, and Morgan Stanley.
Official website: http://www.zxfinance.com

Trust companies: the 65 trust companies across China are essentially arrangers of high yield debts and risky equity products. They are similar to Michael Milken's Drexel Burnham Lambert in the 1980s.

Acknowledgements

I'd like to thank three groups of people.

First, UBS and my former colleagues there. I spent 11 years at UBS in three stints. I met my girlfriend and now wife, Lillian Liu, at UBS. When I was fighting corporate fraudsters such as Greencool Tech and Euro-Asia Agricultural Holdings Company from 2001 to 2002, UBS research management gave me both moral and financial support. I am particularly indebted to Michael Oertli who was Head of Asia Research at the time, Matt Pecot (now at Credit Suisse Group) who was a research product manager at the time, and John Holland, Head of Asia Equity Sales. Oertli hired me back to UBS in 1999 after HSBC had forced me to resign for my honest views on the Chinese government's Yankee Bond issue in December 1998.

(By the way, HSBC take note: I still believe today that the Chinese Yankee Bond deal you did in late 1988 and early 1989 was "a lose-lose proposition"!)

When I spoke out about other issues at UBS as a research analyst — from the Chinese telecom company's caller-part-pays, to the bad behavior of some sneaky companies — UBS always supported me despite complaints from corporate clients.

In 2010, when I was a senior investment banker, I wanted to walk away from a big deal worth many millions of U.S. dollars because of the company management's bad behavior and UBS management supported me once again.

I salute you, UBS!

Second, I'd like to thank my family for their support. While I was in Guangzhou, I told them that everything would be just fine.

Acknowledgements

We have been and continue to be luckier than the vast majority of people around us. They supported me.

And finally, I'd like to thank my editors at Enrich Professional Publishing (Glenn Griffith, Janet Cheng, and Barbara Cao) for their efficient and wonderful editorial work that gave the book a major facelift. Their encouragement has meant a lot to me.

About the Author

Joe Zhang, 50, is an independent corporate advisor based in Hong Kong. From 2011 to 2012, he was Chairman of Wansui Micro Credit Company in Guangzhou, China. He was named "A Microcredit Person of the Year" in January 2012 by the Microcredit Association of China.

He worked for 11 years at UBS, mainly as Head of China Research and then Deputy Head of its China Investment Banking Division.

From 1986 to 1989, he was an official of the central People's Bank of China in Beijing. From 2006 to 2008, he was the Chief Operating Officer of Shenzhen Investment Limited, a property developer.

While Head of China Research at UBS, his team was rated the Number 1 team five years in a row (2001 to 2005), and he personally was rated the Number 1 China Analyst by *Asiamoney* for four consecutive years (2001 to 2004).

Joe received a Master of Economics degree from the Australian National University in 1991, and he taught finance at the University of Canberra from 1991 to 1994.

In the past two decades, his numerous articles have appeared in the *Wall Street Journal*, *Financial Times*, and *International Herald Tribune*. He published two best-selling Chinese books, *The Confessions of a Stock Analyst* and *Avoiding Land Mines in the Stock Market*.

In 2001, while an analyst, he wrote negative research on Greencool Technology and Euro-Asia. Greencool sued Joe in the Hong Kong High Court and the parties eventually settled out of court. Both companies have since gone belly-up and been delisted from the Hong Kong Stock Exchange. The chairmen of both companies eventually served jail time.

About the Sponsor

Haitong International Securities Group Limited

Established in 1973, Haitong International Securities Group Limited ("Haitong International" or "the Group"; Stock Code: 665.HK) is the only overseas business platform of Haitong Securities Co., Ltd. ("Haitong Securities"; Stock Code: 600837.SH; 6837.HK). Haitong Securities is one of the leading securities companies in Mainland China. Leveraging its established advantages in retail broking business, Haitong International is proactively expanding its coverage of corporate finance, asset management, FICC, structured finance, quantitative trading, and wealth management to provide comprehensive financial services to institutional and individual investors domestically and around the globe.

Brokering

The Group provides comprehensive securities brokerage services to over 160,000 global institutional and individual investors including trading in local and global equities and derivatives, bonds, forex and bullion, margin financing, and custodian services. The Group has been named the "Best Equity House in Hong Kong" for 13 consecutive years.

Corporate Finance

Haitong International specializes in the provision of corporate finance and financial advisory services to listed companies and private enterprises worldwide. Services include sponsorship of initial public offerings, underwriting and placing, and financial and compliance advisory. According to Bloomberg, Haitong International ranked second in the market in terms of the number of Hong Kong IPO projects undertaken, and seventh in terms of the underwriting amount in 2012.

Asset Management

Haitong International has extensive asset management experience and offers a full spectrum of investment products and services. In particular, Haitong International has maintained a leading position in the Renminbi business sector and pioneered the successful roll-out of the first RQFII product in early 2012. Haitong International is also the first Mainland-funded institution in Hong Kong to have received QFII and RQFLP qualifications in 2012, rendering the Group the world's only Mainland-funded institution to own all of the RQFII, QFII, and RQFLP qualifications in 2012.

Fixed Income, Currencies, and Commodities

The FICC division was established in early 2012 to strengthen and diversify the Group's income source through proprietary investment and trading in fixed income, currencies, and commodities products. The Group identifies investment opportunities through in-depth analysis and applies conservative strategies to secure financial return.

Structured Finance and Sector Fund

As an innovative business of the Group, the structured investment and finance business has become an important business of Haitong International. The Group has achieved remarkable results in expansion of its pledged finance and structured finance businesses, particularly financing to corporate clients. After obtaining the first RQFLP qualification, the Group has made great strides in its development in the sector fund business, including the setting up of a business team focused on sector fund investment in Mainland China.

With a determined goal to become a world class investment bank, Haitong International is constantly striving for improvement. The wealth management arm of the Group provides a wide array of products and services to meet clients' individual financial targets and needs. In addition to its fee- and commission-based business, the Group has set up Quantitative Trading in recent years to broaden the business scope. With the traditional sell-side businesses being the principal area of operation, the Group also focuses on the development of institutional business and capital-driven innovative business. As the only overseas business platform of Haitong Securities, the Group is well prepared and strives to be a modern and comprehensive investment bank with a leading position in the Greater China region.